For Today's Worship Keybo
Intermediate Level

MW00638212

KEYBOARD WORSHIP
Book 1 of 4

Learn, Integrate, Apply Basic Chords, Voicings, Progressions

DR. BARRY LIESCH

ISBN 978-1-7325764-0-7

Scripture quotations are from the Holy Bible: English Standard Version (ESV) Copyright ©2001 by Crossway, The NIV Study Bible New International Version Copyright ©1985 by Zondervan, and New American Standard Bible (NASB) Copyright ©1973 by Moody Press.

For announcements and more information consult worshipinfo.com

Acknowledgements

I have learned in life that friends are important. And in attempting a mammoth project of this size, a four-book series, friendships are indispensable. This has been especially true for *Book 1*.

In regard to *Book 1*, I am indebted to the following friends, students, and professional keyboardists and colleagues who encouraged me, read chapters, offered feedback, suggested improvements, noted errors, requested clarification, appealed for more "hand holding" ("Please explain more"), and at times (as good friends do) took me to task by putting their finger on gaps and weaknesses: Jeff Askew, Sharon Bernard, George Boespflug, Rachel Brady, Noelle Cablay (major feedback), Debbie Denke, Manami Kawamura, Larry Lawrence, Irene Lee, Jun Lee, Jina Lord, Jon Neal, Rique Pantoja, John Redford, and Jetro da Silva.

After reading chapters, Tom Keene, a seasoned recording artist, strongly urged that a worship band emphasis "definitely" needed to be included. "Ok," I said, "Let's do it." As a result, the band arrangements/performances/charts are Tom's unique contribution. On top of that, Tom's brother, Iam, touched by the ministry mentality motivating the project, professionally mixed over 35 band tracks. Thank you to long-time friends, Tom and Iam! All of the remaining mp3 tracks were created/performed by me.

Moreover, I wish to express my grateful appreciation to Biola University for awarding me a semester sabbatical leave which permitted uninterrupted concentration on the project. Finally, despite technical issues limiting the formatting and physical appearance of the book due to the fixed nature of my PDF chapter files, Charylu Roberts, pianist and founder of O. Ruby Productions, skillfully guided the book through to publication. Thank you, Charylu!

Sharon Bernard graciously proof-read the final drafter and made edits.

Contents

Foreword for Keyboard Series

Learn, Integrate, Apply! I will be at your side as your coach, helping you to grow as a worship keyboardist. In this book, techniques will be explained in detail so you can *learn* them. Listen to the examples. Play them. Get the shapes of the sounds into your fingers! *Integrate* them into your thinking. An abundance of music examples will help you understand how they function in real musical situations. Apply them. Graft them into a favorite worship song, or even better, create an original arrangement.

A major objective of this book and series is to provide you with the tools to build your own musical style (language) for the glory of God.

Intermediate to Advanced Keyboardist. The four books gradually rise in difficulty. *Book 1* begins very, very simply and develops to the intermediate level. It should be useful for a basic, piano proficiency class. Book 2 begins at the intermediate level and morphs to a semi-advanced level. Books 3 and 4 are mostly advanced. In total, about 1200 music examples are presented.

On the whole, these books are aimed at college-level students who have acquired a least *a minimum of two semesters of music theory* (or the equivalent). I expect them to be useful to both undergraduates and graduates. They deal predominantly with harmonic possibilities, which are a foundational building block, and less with rhythm.

Acoustic Piano. The books do not address synthesizer capabilities or idiomatic ways of playing strings, pads, or B3 organ sounds—important! It has grown out of teaching a keyboard lesson in a room with an acoustic keyboard. That's it! However, an extended section is devoted to playing in a worship band (in Books 1 and 2), and accompanying singers and instrumentalists (in Books 3 and 4)..

Detailed Approach, Achievable Chunks, Audio Playback. However, if individuals do not know much music theory and their sight-reading is deficient, the book should still provide solid value. Many examples are very easy to read. The detailed commentary communicates in simple English what is going on musically and theoretically. It breaks down concepts into small, achievable chunks. Audio playback of the examples is included so you can listen and play along, and an extra, special feature will be provided for those who struggle reading music notation (see the end chapter on "What is Midiculous Software?").

Two Kinds of Students. I have been teaching keyboard improvisation at Biola University, an evangelical university of 6000 in the Los Angeles area for many years. Most of my students are music majors whose primary instrument is the piano, undergrads with "classical chops." A good number read music notation fluently. The majority, however, cannot improvise, cannot think in music, do not have a practical grasp of how sounds relate (function with one another), or do so in a simplistic, halting fashion. They don't know what to do. They have not experienced the freedom inherent in improvisation. They are most comfortable with notated music.

On the other hand, I've had other students who improvise well but read music slowly, hesitantly, and with difficulty. The differences between the two, in both background and aptitude, can be startling, extreme! The classical folk read. The improvisers seek to invent. However, the improvisers, too, are limited in their understanding of how music works. They have meager resources and lack the musical concepts to develop their ideas effectively. *This is my attempt to meet the needs of each of these diverse learners.*

Many times, I've gone back to my office after a lesson and have added another step or example to improve clarity. In other words, these materials have undergone much thought, testing, and revision in attempting to "zone in" where students need help.

Problem of Transitory Worship Songs. A major problem concerning the transitory nature of contemporary worship music needs addressing. I appreciate that young people would like the book to contain the very latest, "hot" worship songs. (You'll find some.) But this doesn't make much sense for a book of this sort. Unfortunately, many of the latest songs tend to last a couple of years and they're gone. The "turn over" rate is astonishing, unrelenting. Strange as it may seem, if this book were to major in current worship songs, it would quickly become outdated!

Therefore, I've chosen well-known hymns and worship choruses with a least some proven staying power. However, in actual lessons I have incorporated songs when students exclaim, "I love that song!" These are *their* songs of heart-felt worship. I've learned they are *really* important to them. So, I often respond "Let's look at that song too." It could be an Asian or Latino worship song. Students love this!

Fulfilling a Promise. In another worship book I wrote, *The New Worship: Straight Talk on Music and the Church* (Baker Books, 2001), I called for an outpouring of worship materials in all areas, including music, the dramatic and visual arts, and works that would embrace the theoretical, practical, and pedagogical. I pledged myself to contribute to that effort (p. 35).

These keyboard books are part of my effort to make good on that promise. I want to bless the thirsty keyboardist. If another contributor can borrow from what I have written, improve upon it, and advance the field, terrific! Nothing would make me happier.

No Greater, No Higher Function. Without doubt, many wonderful, marvelous things can be done with music. But I feel confident in declaring this without reservation. There is *no greater, no higher function* for music than to lead people in worship, and to proclaim the eternal Gospel of Jesus Christ.

Ideas in Keyboard Series

In seeking to hone our improvisational capacities, the keyboard has advantages over single-line instruments, for it allows us to think more comprehensively about music—not only melodically but also harmonically. Ideally, we need an…

Abundance of Harmonic Possibilities. We need many options ready at our fingertips. The lyrics may cry out for a precise, fitting sonority. Our chances are much better of finding it if we have an extensive, internalized array of colorful, variegated sounds to draw from. Moreover, the keyboard can help us internalize chord structures and functions. As we make music physically with our fingers, the theory behind music becomes tactile, concrete, alive—less abstract.

Abundance of Examples. The volumes employ over 1200 examples. Three kinds of examples are introduced: (1) abstract examples describe a particular chord and how it functions harmonically; (2) it is then demonstrated a number of times in different songs so you see its potential and usefulness; (3) finally, you'll be given an opportunity to use/apply the technique yourself in a piece where it can function effectively.

Transposition Exercises. The repetition of playing a short phrase, it's functions and spacings over and over again in various keys, helps establish it firmly in our inner ear and fingers. The goal is to acquire the "feel" of chord shapes and relationships so we don't have to think hard about them. A seventh or ninth, for example, has to become as effortless as playing a C major chord.

Transposition greatly stimulates the thinking/hearing process. It tests whether we can apply concepts. It forces us to think in new keys and get "command" of those keys. Transposition assignments are kept short so as to be achievable (often only four measures) and employ well-known songs to make the task more enjoyable and relevant.

Modulation. Once we can play songs in different keys, the desire to be able to fashion effective transitions, and to modulate and to craft segues within and between pieces emerges. Modulations culminating in flowing, seamless worship can usually be handled more competently by keyboardists than guitarists. Therefore we'll offer detailed training in modulation techniques, and we'll discover that sus chords and "four over five" chords are particularly useful.

Chord Spacings (Chord Voicings). Students sometimes have a good idea and may have seized on a good chord progression. However, their realization of it frequently sounds bad. I often ask, "Did that sound good to you? How could we make that same chord, or sequence of chords, sound better? Let's work on that together." The problem is often excessive doubling (even tripling) of notes, particularly in the lower register, and not being sufficiently aware of the inner-voice movement. This book will illustrate many skillful spacing (voicing) options.

Guitar Keys. In worship contexts today, guitarists (who often rule!) tend to avoid keys with flats. They prefer keys with sharps. Therefore, the range of keys in these books is limited to those you will tend to use most frequently. Once we can think in the keys of C, D, E, F, G, and A, it is relatively easy to extend our thinking to the flat keys. Furthermore, this limitation reduces the "brain load," allows us to cover more material, and yet spend sufficient time on the details to truly grasp them.

Sing and Play. The ability to be able to sing and play simultaneously is invaluable when leading or accompanying worship—and it's challenging! It takes extra energy and concentration to maintain good pitch, tone, and congregational eye contact while singing, and yet play fluently and rhythmically, barely looking at the keys. A higher level of keyboard mastery is demanded. We'll be developing this skill. The words to many songs will be provided so you can practice singing and playing.

Collaborate with a Worship Band. This book is also intended to develop your arranging skills so that you can collaborate with a worship band. After exposure to so many rich harmonic possibilities, you will have musical ideas. You'll be able to pitch in and be a creative force. Imagine suggesting during a rehearsal, "How about using this chord? Would this harmonic progression add more interest? Would a modulation between these two songs create a smoother flow?" Moreover, you will be developing skills so you can create your own custom piano arrangements and worship charts.

Creative Ways to Supplement This Book When Teaching

(1) Have students bring in a hymnbook or a photocopy of a song. Added second and sus chords can be penciled in, and 3+1 and 4+2 voicings can be explored.

(2) If you have Asian, African American, or Latino students, encourage them to bring in ethnic pieces.

(3) Prior to the lesson, have students enter on their computers the song lyrics and their original chord progressions. Place the computer or ipad on the piano rack. Expand and enhance what's written. Enter the new pop symbols on the computer immediately.

(4) Have them create an original arrangement of a hymn/song. Encourage them to record on cell phones their ideas and variations immediately as they develop so ideas don't get lost.

(5) Have students record their teacher playing improvised alternatives. This becomes valuable for recall and future reference. It's often difficult to remember what was played.

What Improvisation Requires

Throughout this book I will be at your side as your personal coach, guiding to toward attaining greater competency, so you can serve the Lord confidently in any number of musical situations.

Think for a moment what improvisation requires. Improvisation is speeded-up composition. Improvisation requires knowledge and familiarity with musical processes. Improvisation requires us to "think and live in music" and to fine-tune our "inner ear" so we can imagine, conceive, and bring our ideas to fruition.

Why are many musicians so uncomfortable with improvisation? We frequently find ourselves stuck without ideas. Our processes for fashioning ideas are shallow. Our attempts seem so imperfect and unfinished! Even after we acquire some improvisational knowledge, often we become fixated on the next note in a worship song, *the absolute present,* rather than thinking broadly and freely. Given these challenges, the way we think about improvisation is important. How can be better orient our thinking?

Think of the word I-M-P-A-C-T. Our longing is to impact others for Christ through music. But what does it take? What character and musical qualities do we need?

I Incentive–strong desire–is critical not only to getting started but to sticking with it.

M Musicianship. Artistic sensitivity and a minimum of technical facility is required to perform decently even simple musical ideas. Build your technique! To accomplish this, you will need an acoustic piano or an electronic keyboard with *weighted keys*. When we have an abundance of technique our ideas come more readily.

P Patience—sustained effort—is indispensable. Allowing ourselves time to develop, and a certain willingness to experience trial and error is a precondition for growth.

A Adaptability, being able to work in an ensemble, deal with personalities, read the mood and needs of the congregation is essential. An openness to new styles is part of the improviser's world and required of today's Christian musician.

C Courage, even a certain daring, is crucial for expressing yourself on the spot. This can be scary! We must be able to accept stubbing our toe from time to time. Remember the turtle: *He doesn't make progress until he sticks his neck out.*

T Taste comes from experience and work as well as unteachable instinct. Knowing how much to do or how far to go to enhance worship without distracting from it or calling attention to yourself is a tough call. Sometimes less can be more.

BASIC CHORDS, VOICINGS, PROGRESSIONS

Learning Two Chord Progressions (I–IV–V; I–ii–V)

> • 6 pages
> • 9 examples

OUTLINE	REPERTOIRE
Processes for Beneficial Learning	Father I Adore You
Triads	
Sevenths	

The worship chorus, *Father I Adore You,* contains two *indispensable* chord progressions (I-IV-V-I, and I-ii-V-I). Our goal is to obtain mastery of these two progressions and to pay careful attention to how chords function.

Using simple triads first and then major and minor sevenths, a major objective is also to become competent playing the progressions in different keys. Why? The act of transposition will help us (1) feel/absorb the tactile shapes of the various chord spacings, (2) serve to etch the sounds indelibly in our inner ear, (3) and prompt us to begin to "think in music."

In the next chapter, various strategies for obtaining variety will invite us to "get our hands dirty" and work at integrating techniques. The present chapter begins simply.

Processes for Beneficial Learning

Below, the example is written in C major. Once you can play it fluently in C, we'll learn to play it in the keys, D, E, F, G and A. E and A are favorite guitar keys which occur often in contemporary worship songs.

> **To make your time maximally beneficial,**
> **use your voice to keep your mind engaged:**
>   *a. Call out the bass notes as you play*
>   *b. Call out the pop symbols as you play*
>   *c. Call out the Roman Numerals as you play (most important)*
>   *d. Sing the lyrics as you play*

These techniques will prod you to begin to "think in music."

Triads.

Harmony Restricted to Simple Triads (No Sevenths).

Example 1.1 *Father I Adore You*   Play it!

Notice, the piece is broken down into two progressions that are two measure long: I-ii-V- I occurs twice, and 1-IV-V-I occurs once. All the chords are simple triads.

Roman Numerals. If you don't understand the Roman Numerals written under the bass notes, consult Appendix 2. It explains Roman Numerals and the advantages they have over Pop Symbols. Roman Numerals indicate the *scale degree* on which chords are based, using uppercase for major chords, lowercase for minor chords. (More about them also at the end of the chapter.)

Once you can play the example fluently in C, learn it in D.

Example 1.2 *Father I Adore You.* Use your voice. Keep Focused.

Then move on to the key of G.

Example 1.3 *Father I Adore You.* Play it in G. Call out the Roman Numerals!

Try it! Now close the book (or your eyes) and play *Father I Adore* You in the keys of C, D, G, A.

Sevenths

Below, the same progressions occur in the key of G, but now seventh chords are added.

Example 1.4 Play *Father I Adore You* in G Major. (With Seventh Chords)

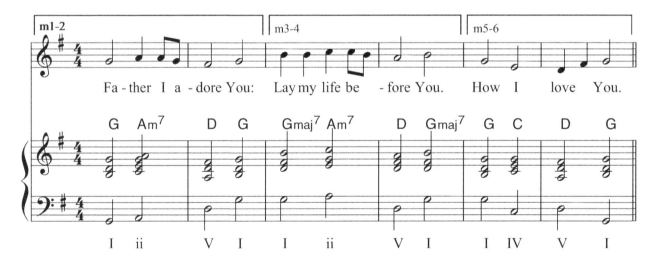

For this chapter, simple Roman Numerals will be used (I -ii -V-I). Even if the ii chord is actually a ii7 (a minor seventh chord), it may be stated as a simple, triadic ii (as in the example below). Why? It allows us to call it out (verbalize it quickly) without complicating verbiage.

Example 1.5 Play *Father I Adore You* in A Major. (With Seventh Chords)

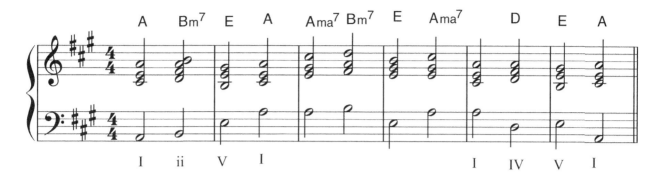

Do it! Close the book (or your eyes). Play *Father I Adore You* in the keys of C, D, G, and A.

Theory Reminders
Note 1. *Don't forget to play the major sevenths*! A major seventh occurs in measure 3 and 4. We want to establish that sound firmly in our ears.

Note 2. *Become comfortable not playing the melody.* The melody is sometimes omitted (let it go). In these beginning examples, I'm generally following the contour of the melody, but not for every note. Maintain smooth chord connections—this is critical! Focus your attention on how the chords function and the harmonies sound to your ear.

Note 3. Parallel fifths and octaves, prohibited in "common practice" classical theory, occur frequently in popular keyboard music. Pay attention to the sound—do the parallel octaves or fifths (see measure one above) sound good?

Note 4. Prod yourself with these questions. How does a ii chord function? How does a IV or V chord function? These are things we need to know when improvising.

Practice Suggestions
1. *Practice each chord progression separately (by memory) in several keys.* Again, the chord progression I- ii-V-I occurs twice. The chord progression I-IV-V-I occurs once. These are essential progressions you need to know really well.

Example 1.6 Play *Father I Adore You* in F Major. (With Seventh Chords)

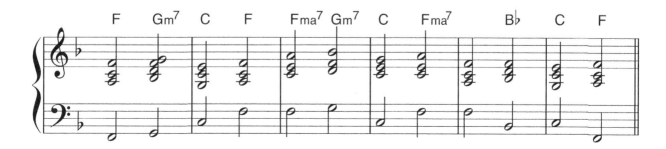

Example 1.7   I-ii -V-I in F, G, and A Major
              (Extracted progression from measures 1 & 2)

Play the above progression in the keys of C, D, E, F, G, and A major.

Example 1.8 Variant Voicing of I-ii-V-I in F, G, and A Major
              (Extracted progression from measures 3 & 4)

Play the progression in the keys of C, D, E, F, G, and A major.

Example 1.9 I-IV-V-I in F, G and A Major
              (Extracted progression from measures 5 & 6)

Play it in the keys of C, D, E, F, G, and A major.

2. *Practice the progressions until you can perform the entire piece fluently.* If this is challenge, divide the piece into segments. Concentrate on the first two measures, then the first four together, and then play the full six measures as a unit. Divide and conquer.

3. *Close the book!* Play the song by memory. Let the chord patterns guide your thinking.

What We've Learned. We've learned that a ii chord can progress to a V chord, a IV chord to a V, and a V to a I. We worked on getting the feel of that into our fingers in different keys. We learned to think in a few keys.

Roman Numerals. Roman Numerals are exceptionally helpful in learning to "think in music." Whereas Pop Symbols describe a chord situated in a *particular* key (e.g., F major chord in the key of C or Bb), Roman Numeral relationships are effectual for *all* keys. For instance, the Roman Numeral "ii" (indicating a minor chord on scale degree two) has the function of ii on scale degree two in every key. The Pop Symbol F major, however, is scale degree four in the key of C, but scale degree five in the key of Bb. It's function can vary with each key. It does not purport, in itself, to indicate any function. It is a description of itself.

The Roman Numeral concept is broader, more comprehensive, and efficient. *Numbers have special properties*. They can relate to one another. Using Roman Numerals, we can talk about chords that are a third apart (I-vi-IV), or a fifth apart (vi-ii-V-I), and that description holds good for *each and every* key. Roman Numerals reveal patterns, relationships, and indicate functions whereas Pop Symbols do not.

Next Chapter
In the next chapter we'll play *Father I Adore You* twelve different ways, using (for the most part) the very same progressions. Twelve different strategies for improvising with the chords will be shared.

> *By wisdom a house is built,*
> *and through understanding, it is established;*
> *through knowledge its rooms are filled*
> *with rare and beautiful treasures.*
> Proverbs 24:3, 4

Ways to Play the Two Progressions

- 15 pages
- 32 examples

OUTLINE	REPERTOIRE
9 Strategies for Developing Variety	Father I Adore You
3 More Strategies for Developing Variety	

The two progressions, I-IV-V and I-ii-V, are still center stage. As the chapter develops, 12 different ways to obtain variety will be shared. You'll be invited to "get your hands dirty" and work at integrating the techniques.

The chapter is intended to appeal to both the intermediate and advanced keyboardist. It begins very simply, but several advanced examples toward the end provide a foretaste ("teasers") of ideas found in volumes two and three—musical ideas you may find intriguing.

9 Strategies for Developing Variety

1. Change the voicing. Compare the Am7 with the seventh in the tenor and then the alto.

Example 2.1 The Seventh is in the Tenor and then the Alto. Play in F, G, and A.

Am7 is a ii7 chord in the key of G

The first chord above is warmer, right? Using the seventh in the left hand is a secret for unlocking nice harmonic colors, as long as the sevenths are not in a really low register. When really low (a fifth lower than the above chord), they become muddy.

Example 2.2 Warmer Voicings for Major and Minor Sevenths (see Asterisks)

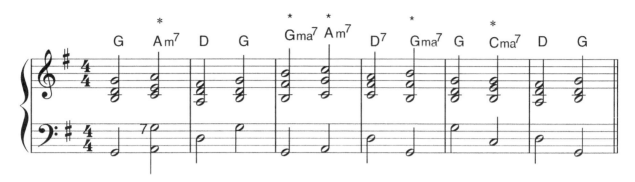

Try it! Play this warmer version in the keys of F, G, and A. If that's difficult, break it into 2 measure phrases. Notice the new spacings in ms. 1, 3, 4, and 5.

So far the progressions have been relatively static. Let's create some movement.

2. *Create Movement in the Bass**. (Bass players often use similar patterns.)*

Example 2.3 Continue the Pattern to the End.
            Then Repeat it: Add Seventh Chords in the key of F

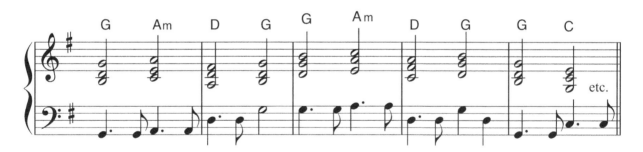

Example 2.4 Create Your Own Bass Pattern (Or Vary the Pattern Below)

3. *Create a Rocking Motion*

Example 2.5 Which Sounds Better?

The wider spacings (those on the right side) result in a warmer sound.

Example 2.6 Rocking Motion Accompaniment. Play it.

4. Try an Interlocking Two-Handed Arpeggiation. Create a continuous arpeggio that transfers from hand to hand (as below).

Example 2.7 Hand-to-Hand Arpeggiation

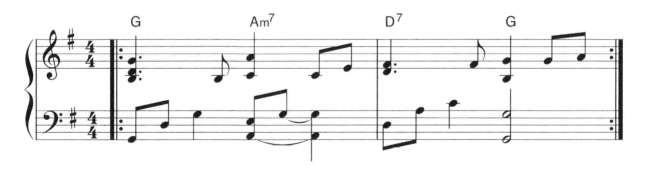

5. Ways to Employ a Pedal Bass

Example 2.8 The Bass Part Stays on C

Example 2.9 Soprano Part has Pedal on C and G.

6. Syncopated Version

Example 2.10 Play in G and A.

7. Create a Rock Version

Example 2.11 Rock Feel. Play it in G and A major.

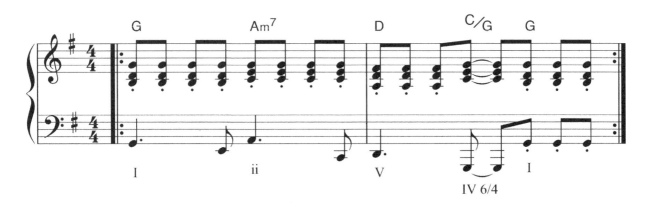

A *slash symbol* (m.2) is introduced for the first time. Did you notice the C/G symbol? It means: play a C chord in you RH and a single note (G) in the bass with your LH.

The IV chord (m.2) is a C chord. The Symbol "6/4" indicates a second inversion chord with the fifth of the C chord (G) played in the bass. The 6 and the 4 indicate a sixth and fourth occur above the bass note. Again, for more information on Roman Numerals, consult Appendix2.

8. Create a Syncopated Arpeggiated Pattern

Example 2.12 Soprano Part follows the Melody. Quarter Notes in Bass. Play in G and A.

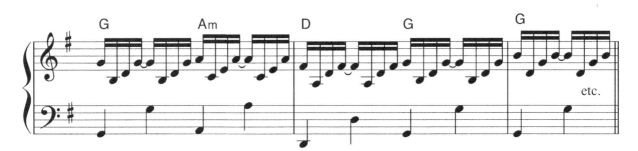

Example 2.13 Flowing Guitar-Like Pattern

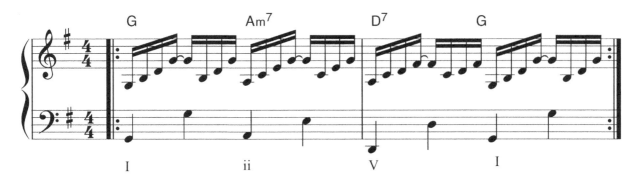

Play it! Can you discern how the pattern is organized? Focus on the lowest RH note in every group of four-sixteenth notes. The basic pattern (six measures) is worked out below. Can you sing it while playing the syncopation in your RH? Tricky.

Example 2.14 Play Through the Piece Using the Sixteenth Note Accompaniment.

Example 2.15 Flowing Guitar-Like Pattern in A Major. Play the 6 measures.

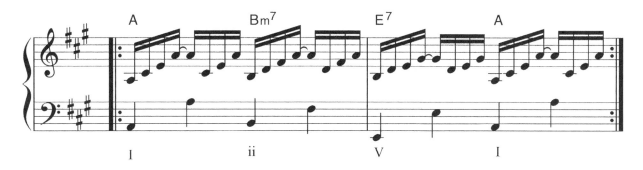

Try it! Repeat the excerpt several times. Then continue the pattern through to the end of the piece in A major. This takes technique. Use it to develop your technique.

9. *Arpeggiate the Chord Progressions*

Example 2.16 Arpeggiated Version. *(Father I Adore You)*

Let's look at four ways to arpeggiate.

Example 2.17 Four Arpeggiated Chord Alternatives

Try it! Work through the first three patterns above—for the first 4 measures of *Father I Adore You.*

Now let's develop the last pattern above (measure 4). Note the rest in the left hand and the 10ths outlining the bass pattern. When applied to the first four chords of *Father I Adore You*, it has a more flowing character.

Example 2.18 Left Hand of Flowing Variation (outlines up a tenth)

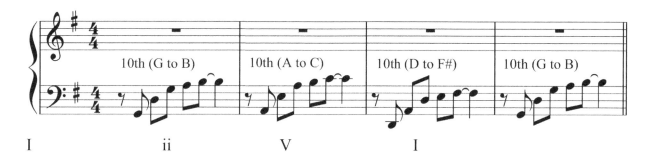

Try it! Play this pattern in the keys of D, E, and G.
Now let's add the right hand to the flowing left hand.

Example 2.19 Play it in the keys of D, E, F, G, and A.

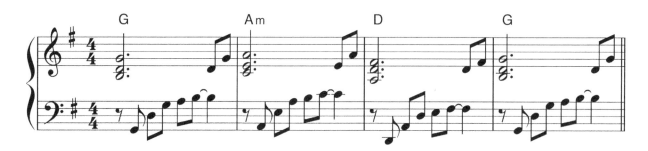

Try it! Once you have mastered it, don't feel you must follow this pattern slavishly. The result could become excessively rigid and boring. Vary the pattern. Alternate it with one of the others.

3 More Strategies for Developing Variety

The next three strategies are more intricate: (1) ornament the melody; (2) use open spacings (wide chord voicings); (3) change the harmonies.

1. Ornament the Melody

Ornaments introduce melodic flourishes into the melody. They are not "basic" structure, but the "extras" — like blossoms on the branches of trees. Below, the eighth and sixteenth notes function as melodic ornaments. **Do it!** Ornament the entire melody.

Example 2.20 Simple Ornamentation *(Father I Adore You)*

©1987 Terrye Strom   All Rights Reserved. Used by Permission.

Example 2.21 More Rhythmically Subtle Ornamentation *(Father I Adore You)*

Choose a slower tempo. This is an illustration to show ornamentation can be complex.

Example 2.22 The Subtle Version Harmonized *(Father I Adore You).* Play Slowly.

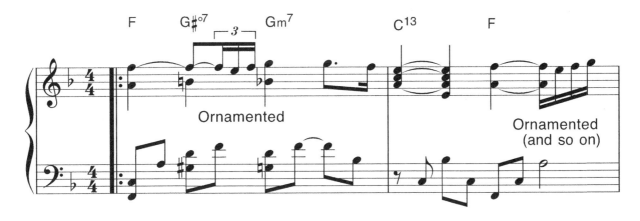

2. Use Open Spacings (Wide Chord Voicings). Open spacings unlock a contrasting category of colors.

Example 2.23 Arpeggiated Tenths in the Left Hand

Observe, the RH has open spacings. When arpeggiating in a low register, the LH intervals need to be wide (octaves, fifths, or sixths). Avoid low thirds (they sound muddy). In m.1, the LH broken chords begin on the downbeat. But notice the rhythmic change in m. 3 where the LH (on the offbeat) follows after the RH. This variation creates energy, provides rhythmic variety, and avoids monotony.

Try it! Practice having the LH follow the RH. Students find this takes effort before it becomes natural. So revise the example. Lead with your RH for the entire example. Below are a few measures to get you started.

Example 2.24 LH Follows the RH

Example 2.25 Arpeggiated Ninths in Left Hand (see asterisks).

3. Change the Harmonies. The more sophisticated harmonic variations below are intended to give a taste of what is possible. "Q" indicates a chord comprised of perfect fourths (a quartal chord).

Example 2.26 Experience the Alternative Harmonies

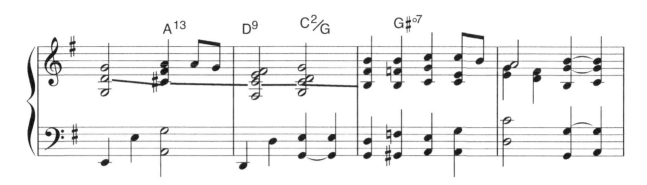

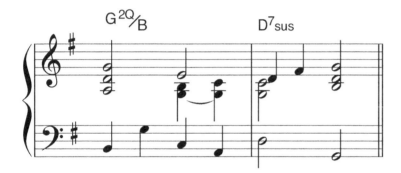

How was that created? Full-blown explanations will have to wait for another time. For now though, note that the first two measures have descending fifths in the bass (E - A - D - G), a well-known pattern (vi - II - V - I). See a simplified version immediately below. We'll use that pattern again with the hymn *Amazing Grace* (chapter 4).

Example 2.27 Descending Fifths Simplified Harmonically

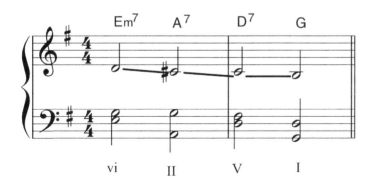

The alto part falls chromatically by half steps. The bass continues a series of descending fifths (down a fifth, up a fourth).

Example 2.28 Experience Another Harmonic Alternative

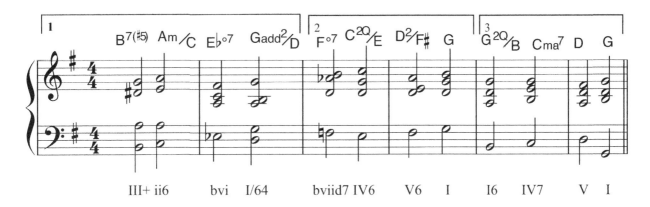

See the added second chords (Gadd2/D, D2/F#) and quartal chords (C2Q/E, G2Q/B). Added Second chords and Quartal chords are addressed in detail in Volume Two. A chord catalogue is available in the Appendix.

Try it! Play the example above with wide broken chords in the LH (as below).

Example 2.29 Wide Broken Chords *(Father I Adore You)*

Try it again! This time play the same sonorities but with solid chords (roll them as needed). Principle: if the solid chords sound good, then the broken chords will too.

To get great sounds, experiment doubling different notes. Do the doublings sound good? Do they fall easily for your hand? Or, avoid doubling altogether: make each note unique. How you space chords matters!

Above, did you notice that major second intervals were employed seven times? Play the awkward ones using your thumb on both notes (see first two chords). The seconds contributed a "crunch" to the sounds. Did you like that effect? To omit the added seconds and obtain a cleaner, purer sound, delete the notes A and B in the first two chords.

Example 2.30 Experience Another Harmonic Variation

Explanation. In creating the first two measures, I was looking for a path to the goal note, the bass note "B" (bass movement from E to B). More importantly, once the Fmaj7 (m.3) was found (happy discovery!) the descending fifths quickly occurred to me. Once you become familiar with using a series of descending fifths, they will spontaneously occur to you. You'll hear them. The "descending fifths" beginning in m. 3 (C-F-B-E-A-D-G) unify this passage harmonically. A sense of longing was intended in the alto part (m. 5). Was it successful?

Example 2.31 Series of Descending Fifths (Down a Fifth = Up a Fourth)

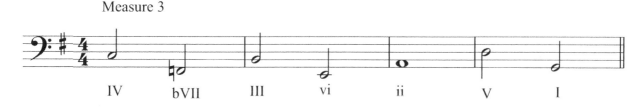

Try it! Can you play the harmonic alternative in F and A major? It is challenging. (Volume Three addresses descending fifths, so important, in detail.)

Try it! Play all three harmonic versions continuously with the second version using broken chords. If you were to play the three variations as the chorus was sung in church three times, would the people experience the worship differently?

Interlude. Time for a break, a change of routine! Play the lead sheet below as is. Then, *come up with three variations.* Try out the various techniques covered in the chapter. Arpeggiate the chords? Create some bass movement, some rocking motion, or use a pedal? Ornament the melody? Use wide spacings? Change the harmonies?

Example 2.32 **Improvise!** (Lead Sheet)

Next Chapter
In the next chapter we return to basics and take a look at ii and IV in V-I cadences.

> ***A Way to Increase Your Motivation.***
> Write out your identity as a worship keyboardist.
> Clarify what you would like to be and do.
> Compose short statements. For example…
> *I am a triumph maker.*
> *I stir up the people to sing with energy and conviction.*
>
> *I help the people feel the truth.*
> *I help people draw close to God.*
>
> *I "text paint."*
> *I play close attention to the words and imagery in hymn and choruses.*
> *I help people discover new meanings buried in songs.*
>
> *I try to bring some freshness into the situation.*
> *I help the service to flow.*
>
> These objectives appeal to me personally.
> Compose several statements of your own.
> Write them down using your own words and turns of phrases.

Back to Basics

- 7 pages
- 19 examples

OUTLINE	REPERTOIRE
ii, IV in V-I Cadences	Be Thou My Vision Holy Holy Holy
vi in V-I Cadences	How Great Thou Art God is So Good
Voicing Chords Across the Keyboard	As the Deer Great is Thy Faithfulness

ii, IV in V-I Cadences

We return to basics. In using *Father I Adore You* in the previous chapter, the ii chord occurred at the *beginning* of phrases. The ii chord, however, is often employed at the *end* of V-I Cadences. We need to reinforce that. Furthermore, let's compare the ii and IV chords at V-I cadences. Finally, the vi chord is introduced. To fix the progressions firmly in our minds and ears, we'll connect them with a well-known worship song.

Each example is in the key of G. Transpose each into the keys of A, G, F, and E.

Example 3.1 *How Great Thou Art*   ii V I   Play in the Keys of A,G,F,E.

Example 3.2 *How Great Thou Art*   IV V I   Play in the Keys of A,G,F,E.

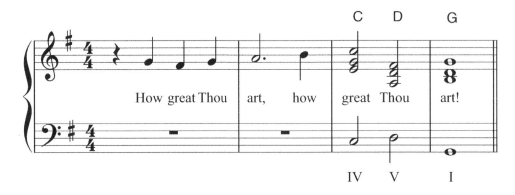

Example 3.3 *Be Thou My Vision*   ii IV/5 I   Play in the Keys of A,G, F, E.

Example. 3.4 *Be Thou My Vision*   IV IV/5 I Play in the Keys of A, G, F, E

Example 3.5 *As the Deer*   ii V I.   IV V I   Play in the Keys of A, G, F, E.

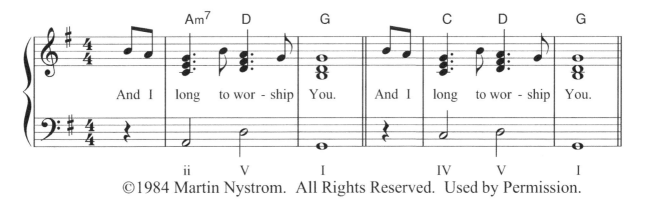

vi in V-I Cadences

Chords on scale degree vi occur often in traditional and contemporary worship songs. The vi chord often leads to a ii chord first, before proceeding to the V and I.

Example 3.6 *Holy Holy Holy* I vi ii V I Play in C, D, and E.

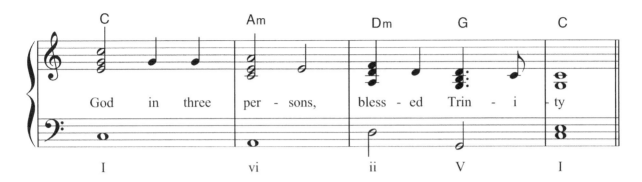

The vi-ii-V-I progression (above) results in a down a 5th, up a 4th movement in the bass.

Example 3.7 *Great is Thy Faithfulness* I vi ii V I Play in C, D, E.

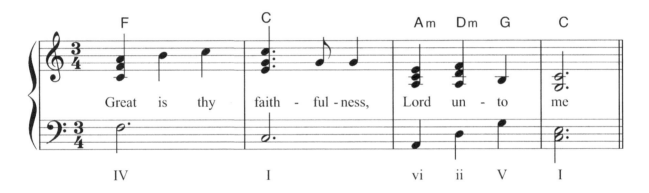

Example 3.8 Silent Night I vi ii V I   Play in C and D.

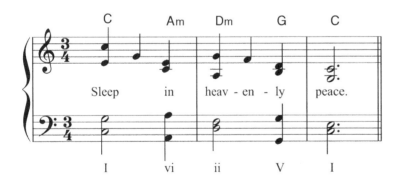

Example 3.9   Holy Holy Holy   I vi V I   Play in Keys of C, D, E, F.

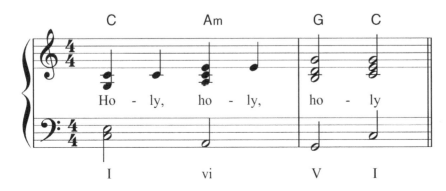

Example 3.10 *Amazing Grace*   vi I V I   Play in G, F, and E.

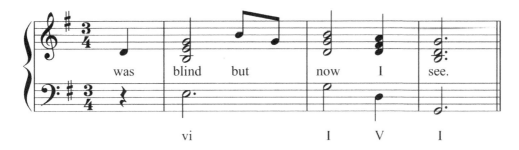

Example 3.11   Be Thou My Vision   I vi IV I   Play in G, F, E and D.

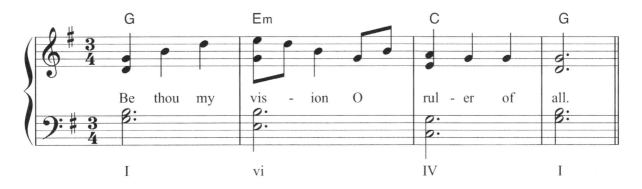

Notice the "descending thirds" pattern in the bass. This occurs frequently.
We have now worked on cadences that involve ii, IV, and vi, three essential chords.

Voicing Chords Across the Keyboard

Don't become stuck playing *only* in the middle of the keyboard (I see this often). Utilize
the high and low registers especially in climactic passages. Contrast is vital!
Below, the keyboard is divided into low, middle, and high areas.

Example 3.12 the Preferred sounds Across the Keyboards

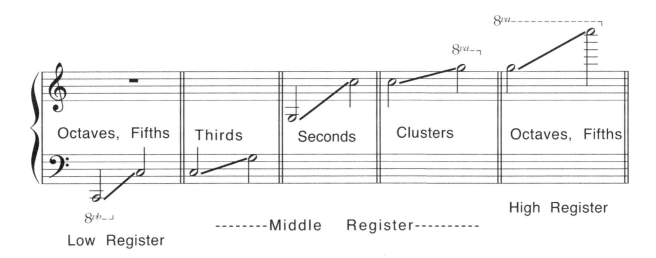

The middle register is your blending area. Any interval can sound good — this is the place to use seconds, thirds, and sevenths. The moderately high register is excellent for clusters of notes. The extreme low end is powerful. The extreme high end is capable of cutting through textures. Open sounds such as fifths and octaves work the well in the extreme upper and lower edges of the keyboard for forte passages.

Let's illustrate the concept using four similar chords with D as the melody note on top.

Example 3.13

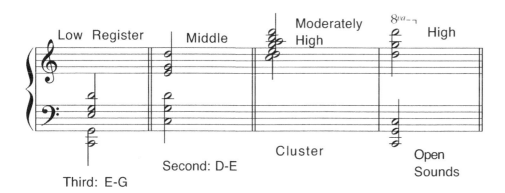

Above, the third (E-G) in measure one is in a good range, as is the second (D-E) in measure two. The clusters (m.3) obtain a nice sheen in the moderately high register, and open sounds (m.4) work well in the extreme high and low registers.

Avoid muddy sounds. Thirds and sevenths sound muddy in low registers. Unless you intentionally want a dark sound, instead use fifths, octaves, tenths—even sixths can sound good providing they are not really low.

Example 3.14

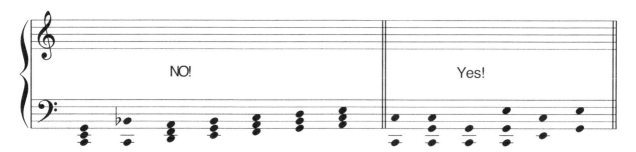

For instance, below the excerpt of *Be Thou My Vision* below has muddy thirds.

Example 3.15 *Be Thou My Vision*

If you have a limited keyboard technique and must use block chords in your left hand, employ them in and around middle C. Raise the melody an octave if necessary.

Example 3.16 Left Hand an Octave Higher Avoids Muddiness

For a thicker, warmer sound, use wide tenths in the bass (measure one below). Or, for a more sturdy sound use a combination of octaves and fifths (measures three to five).

Example 3.17 Warmer (m. 1), Sturdier (ms. 2-4)

If you are playing in a band, usually there's no need to play the melody.

Example 3.18 Synth Pad for *Be Thou My Vision (No Melody)*

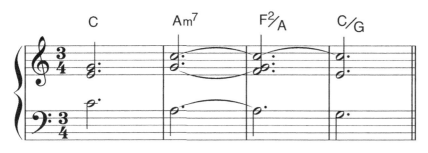

The ties help create a sense of smoothness.

When creating a pad or string part on a synthesizer (as above) consider using open spacings, common tones (ms 2-4), and inversions that result in linear lines (i.e., see the bass and the alto movement E-G-F-E). It's not mandatory to play the bass notes in measures three and four, since the bass player is probably covering that area.

Also, a single, linear, string line (without any harmony) can be effective. For example, string parts for the chord progression above could look like this. It could be performed an octave higher too.

Example 3.19 Possible String Line

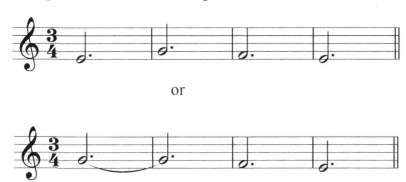

or

Worship While You Perform.
This is not always easy in actual practice.
You are busy thinking, executing, listening, singing.
The better you master your music each week,
the freer you'll feel to worship.
Even an ant can awaken us to the necessity of preparation.

Go to the ant, O sluggard,
observe her ways and be wise,
which having no chief, officer, or ruler,
prepares her food in the summer,
and gathers her provision in the harvest.
Prov 6:6-8

Ways to Play *God Is So Good* and *Amazing Grace*

- 14 pages
- 24 examples

OUTLINE	REPERTOIRE
Basic Version	God is So Good
More Expressive Version	Amazing Grace
More Sophisticated Possibilities	

Chapters one and two were intended to lay a foundation so you can be successful with this chapter, which will require more understanding. Learn to play *God is so Good* and *Amazing Grace* in various ways and keys using a Lead Sheet and a Roman Numeral chart. We'll begin very simply, but the material will develop considerably.

Basic Version

Learn to play the six examples of *God is so Good* in the keys of C, D, E, F, G, and A. First, play *only* the melody in all the keys. This will free you up to focus on other elements later.

Example 4.1 *Melody of God is So Good* Play in C, D, E, F, G, and A.

Now play the bass and melody notes together.

Example 4.2 Melody & Bass of *God is So Good.* Play it in C, D, E, F, G, A.

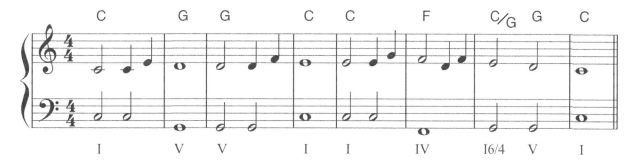

Try it! Close the book (or your eyes).

Below, in fleshing out the harmonies, we'll use the *3+1 voicing* (discussed in detail in chapter 11). A three-note chord occurs in the RH, one note in the LH (bass). For some melody notes, use single notes rather than chords. After you play it in a few different keys, it gets easier. Be encouraged!

Example 4.3 Basic Harmonization of *God is So Good*   Play in C, D, E, F, G, and A

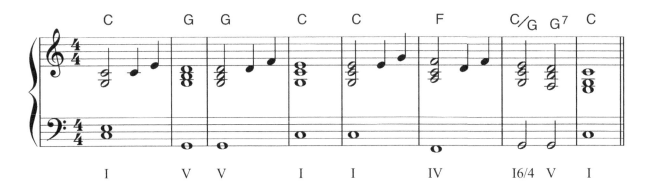

Example 4.4 More Ideas for Playing *God is So Good*   Play in C, D, E, F.

A. Two New Wrinkles: (1) ii-V-I; (2) V of ii

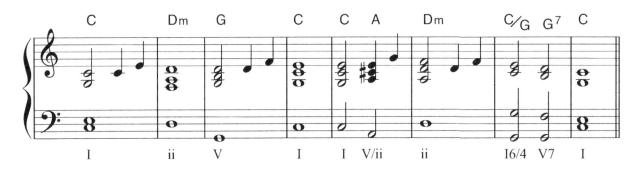

In measures 2-4, a ii-V-I chord progression occurs. In measures 6-8, essentially the same thing happens (with the I6/4 preceding the V7).

Explanation of "secondary dominants." The A chord in measure 5 is called a "secondary dominant." A dominant chord is a V chord and all dominant progressions have a V-I movement. A "primary" dominant progression (if we can use that expression) occurs when the I chord is on scale degree 1 of the key. For example, the V-I progression in measures 7-8 ends on scale degree 1 of C major. Indisputably, that particular progression, used in that way, is the most powerful of all the music progressions in Western music.

However, what if the V-I idea could be expanded conceptually? What if a V-I progression could be applied to a scale degree other than I? For example, what if we could have a V of scale degree ii, iii, IV, and so on. Look! Measure 5 has a V of ii. When thus expanded, the V-I is called a "secondary dominant" because it is secondary in function to the more primary V- I progression that ends on scale degree 1.

Secondary dominants tend to function as energizers. Chromaticism (notes outside the basic scale) invariably results. Notice the C# in measure 5. Did the A chord contribute energy to the phrase? Did it add spice to the harmonization? Did you like the "happy" A major sound? Clearly, an A major chord on scale degree 6, is brighter than the A minor chord, which normally occurs on scale degree 6.

Secondary dominants are tools we can use when arranging and improvising. In book 3, we spend an entire chapter showing ways to apply them. The concept is capable of substantial development. A V7, V9, or V13, or some other V alteration could substituted. The I chord could be major or minor, even include an extension. A series of V-I progressions could be fashioned.

A question for you. A important goal of this book is to help you "think in music." Did our lengthy, secondary dominant explanation help you understand what we mean when we talk about "thinking in music"?

B. Two more wrinkles: (1) inner-voice movement; (2) V7 of IV.

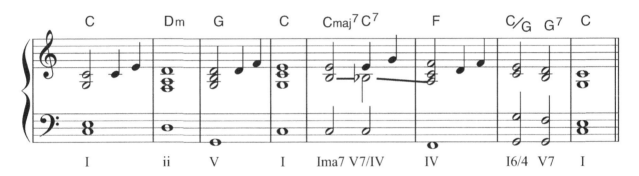

Explanation. The V7 of IV (m.5) is also a ***"secondary dominant,"*** a dominant chord is "applied" to the IV chord (instead of the I chord on scale degree 1). Also, did you like the smooth, inner-voice movement in the alto (B – Bb – A)? Did it contribute some feeling? Inner-voice movement can be beautiful, expressive—another big idea.

Improvise! *Create two variations.* Now that you have learned the block chords for the various keys, and two other ways to embellish the song, slow down. Improvise. Take some time. Create some variety. Make the piece sound more expressive. Ornament the melody, add sevenths, use arpeggios, wider spacings, employ some rocking motion, and so on. However, limit yourself to the basic chord structure (progressions) provided.

Now do the same, below, in the key of E. This harmonization allows for inner-voice movement. Can you create it? Also compare the band version of *God is So Good* in chapter 15.

Example 4.5 Play and then Improvise Upon the Lead Sheet Version *(God is So Good)*

Amazing Grace. You will have many opportunities to play *Amazing Grace.* It's probably the most famous hymn in North America! Therefore, we will want to learn it well and invent interesting ways to play it. Improvise on the simple chart below. (We'll develop this more shortly.)

Example 4.6 **Improvise!** 4/4 Version of *Amazing Grace*   Play in D, E, F, G, and A

Example 4.7 Improvise in 3/4 Time. *Amazing Grace*

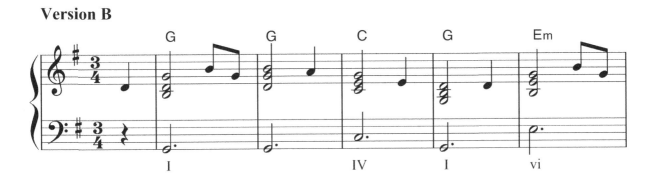

Example 4.8 Improvise in 4/4 Time. Play in D, E, F, G and A

Amazing Grace is often played with a triplet feeling (a shuffle feeling). ***Try it.***
Experiment with triplets.

In the demonstration below, see a "shuffle" version (Compare it with chapter 17 where
the band also plays a shuffle version). Shuffle rhythms are meant to swing. The triplets
help the piece swing. Do you also sense a 9/8 feeling? A few harmonic liberties are
taken, but the chart stays pretty much the same. Melodic ornamentation occurs.

Example 4.9 Shuffle Version (Swings) *Amazing Grace*

Do it! First, play the above notation as is. For the repeat, come up with your own variation, your own ornaments, etc. Does your version develop, expand upon, what was written? Would it stimulate listener attentiveness? Try to make the song flow, move.

Explanation of Cadences. In chapter two we talked about *V - I cadences* (also termed "full," "authentic, or "perfect" cadences). They generally have a feeling of finality, completeness, or closure, as occurs in m.16 above. Notice, the familiar descending fifth pattern (vi → II → V → I) also contributes to a secure close. (More on that shortly.)

On the other hand, ***"Half cadences"*** (also termed "imperfect" cadences) end on the Roman Numeral V (not I). A half cadence occurs on measure 7. Half cadences generally convey a sense of incompleteness, as if they are "half way" done, and lack a sense of resolution. If you listen carefully to the piece as a whole, you should definitely be able to experience how differently the half and full cadences function.

Sus Chords. Sus chords are extremely valuable at cadence points (see the Dsus9, m.7). They can be used to create harmonic colors at cadence points, even extend the cadence. They have many uses. Sus chords do not have a third in the chord. Instead they have a fourth (see the G in the Dsus9 chord). Volume Two devotes three chapters to sus chords, explaining them in detail, as they lend themselves to extended development, and are a big part of contemporary music. (More on sus chords below.)

More Expressive Version

Before attempting the more expressive version of *Amazing Grace (further down below)*, we need to flesh out and work on some of the more difficult chord symbols, the augmented chords, as well as the alternative spacings for the sus9 chords, which are employed at two cadence points.

Example 4.10 Augmented Seventh, B7(#5), in First Phrase of *Amazing Grace*

Above in measure 2, see the augmented chord in the right hand (B, D#, G) and the minor seventh in the left hand (A). A major triad on B would be B, D#, F#. The G raises or augments the F sharp, thus the term "augmented chord." Technically, the G is an F double sharp, but a G is written for easy reading. In measure 3, a major second (D) is added to the C chord. Below, the chromatic movement from D to D# to E in the alto part.

Example 4.11 Chromatic Movement Highlighted. Play in E, F, G, and A.

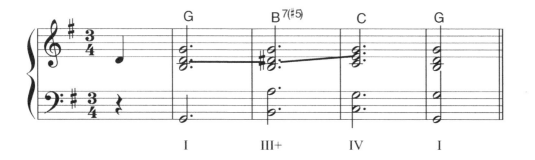

Now let's look at two sus alternatives to the dominant seventh at the half cadence.

Example 4.12 Second Phrase. Two Sus9 Alternatives at the Half Cadence

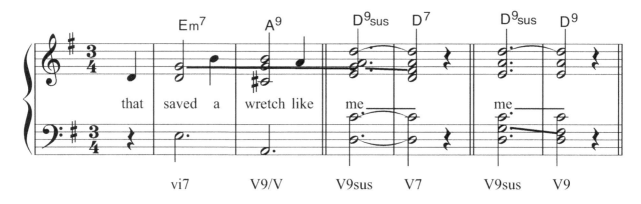

Observe how smoothly the parts move. In the first four measures above, the G (common tone) is retained and then resolves to F#. Generally, we want things to fall naturally and easily for our hands, and retaining common tones helps that process.

In the last two measures above, the sus9 is revoiced with perfect 4ths in the right hand (a "quartal" sound), and the sus resolves in the LH (G to F#). Do you like this effect? Let's proceed to the full cadence.

Example 4.13 Last Phrase. Three Sus9 Alternatives at the Full Cadence

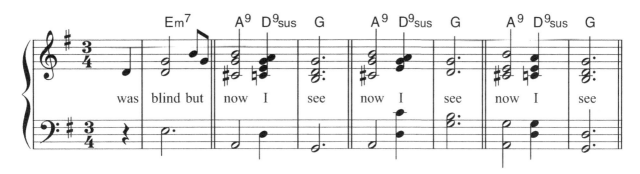

Above, the first two D9sus chord have changes in the fingering. The third statement, however, has a different spacing (voicing)— it's warmer. Notice too, that the bass falls in a series of descending fifths (vi-II-V-I), a secure progression. Another observation: the alto/tenor part falls chromatically from D to C# to C to B (see below).

Example 4.14 Chromatic Descent of the Alto/Tenor Line

These two factors—the bass and the chromatic descent in the alto and the descending fifths in the bass—form an essential part of the inner, musical logic.

Example 4.15 Bare Bones Structure. Play in the keys of D, E, F, G, and A.

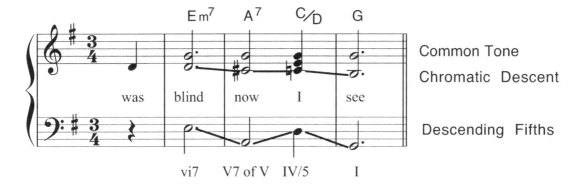

Try it! Remember to play the phrase above in the keys of D, E, F, G, and A!
Below, we'll delay the alto/tenor descent by employing a 4-3 suspension. And in order to provide more resonance, we'll also add a 13th (B) to the sus sonority.

Example 4.16 4-3 Suspension in Measure 2

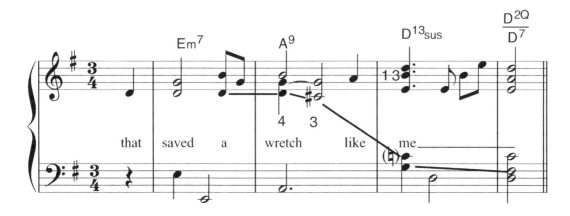

Do it! Now (below) integrate all of the above variations, paying special attention to the half and full cadence areas (ms. 5-8; 13-16) of *Amazing Grace.* Make up your own stuff for measures 9-12.

Example 4.17 **Improvise!** More Complex Version of *Amazing Grace*

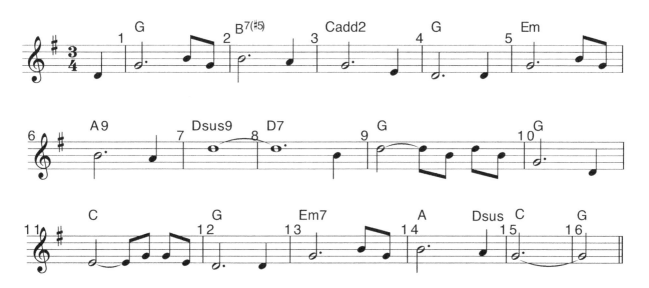

The version in C major (below), expressed in a *Roman Numeral format*, has the augmented chord we used previously, III+(7). To get oriented and prepared, play the next example.

Example 4.18 E7(#5) in Key of C.

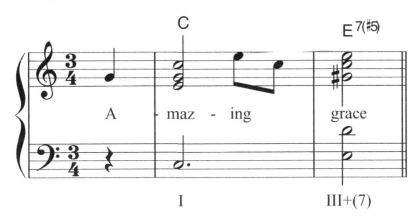

Example 4.19 Version of *Amazing Grace* (Roman Numeral Chart)

The II9 chords (lines 2 & 4) are theoretically termed V of V (secondary dominants) but Roman Numeral II more directly guides us to the right scale degree. Roman Numerals convey chord function (solidifying and clarifying our thinking process). Play *Amazing Grace* in the keys of C, D, E, F, G , and A using Roman Numerals.

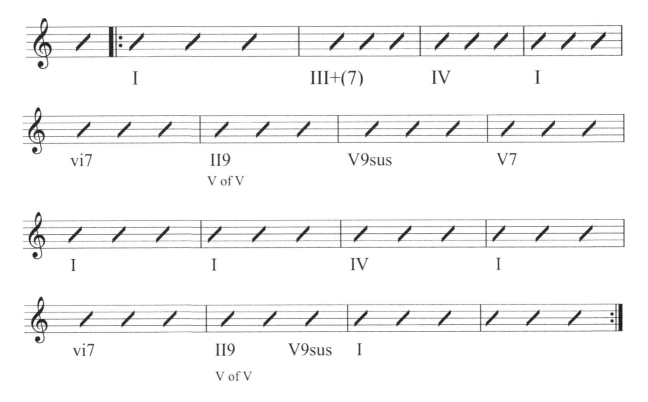

We will discover in Volume Three that several formulations of the vi - ii - V - I progression are possible. Roman Numerals help us think functionally.

More Sophisticated Possibilities

This section is quite a leap in harmonic difficulty! You are not expected to come up with stuff like this now. However, I wanted to give you at least a taste of more sophisticated harmonic possibilities—things we'll explore in Volumes Two and Three. For instance, you may want to "open up" the chords we used previously. So let's widen the voicing/spacing of the III7(#5) and V9sus sonorities.

Example 4.20 Widening the Augmented Sound (#5)

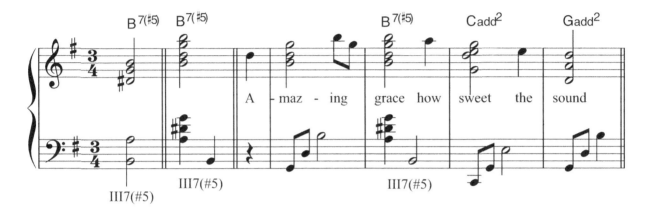

In measure two of *Amazing Grace* [B7(#5) chord], the right hand, technically, should have had a D#, which would have resulted in a D# doubling with the left hand. However, I liked the subtle B-B# tension. Try it both ways.
Let's turn to the sus9 chord. Below, two sus9 chords are used in a row (see asterisks).

Example 4.21 Two Consecutive Sus9 Chords

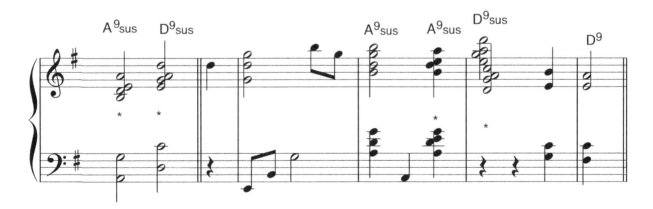

The last chord above is a rootless D9.

Below, the thirteenth added to the sus chord creates even more color. Moreover, it's spacing is much wider (roll it). Yet the composite sound is quite similar to the sus9.

Example 4.22 Sus13

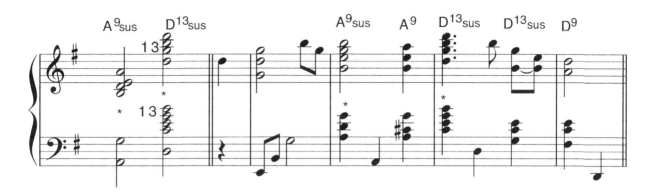

Example 4.23 Create Your Own Version of *Amazing Grace*

Idea: borrow material from any of the examples in this chapter, and integrate them alongside of your own stuff. Come up with a finished product that represents your best effort. To differentiate this effort from the previous shuffle improvisation, avoid triplets. Use straight eighths and sixteenths.

For comparison purposes, see the version below.

Example 4.24 The Finale! Applying the Ideas. (Amazing Grace)

Something like the dynamic build up in measures 11 and 12, and the intimate retard in 13-16, can actually be accomplished during congregational worship singing if someone conducts the people skillfully. Don't under estimate the people! The "congregational choir" can learn to respond with sensitivity. For many, the resulting newness of expression can be not only delightful but deeply meaningful.

The Control Center. A theologian-friend of mine wrote a book on the heart. He called the heart "the control center." Insightful?

When worshiping, is your music coming from your heart? Is your heart drawing you to work on this book?

> *Whatever you are doing,*
> *put your whole heart into it,*
> *as if you were doing it for the Lord*
> *and not for men.*
> *Col 3:23*

Major and Minor Triad Patterns

- 14 pages
- 24 examples

OUTLINE	REPERTOIRE
Practicing Inversions	Joyful, Joyful We Adore Thee
Closed and Open Voicings	Give Thanks Spirit Song
Pachelbel Cannon (Down a 4th, Up a 5th)	Be thou My Vision
Progressions Down a 5th, Up a 4th	Revelation Song
Practicing the Cycles	Jesus, Name Above All Names

This chapter addresses two ways of spacing or "voicing" chords: closed, and open. We'll also look at harmonic progressions that descend a 4th and a 5th. For best results, learn these chord patterns in all keys or at least the "white" keys. This will help you develop the tactile feeling/shape of chords and metal agility leading to confident fluency.

If you do not know the major scale in all the keys, master that first. Find a book that provides you with the correct fingerings —here are the fingerings for a couple of keys.

Example 5.1 Major Scale in Keys of C and Db

Practicing Inversions

Example 5.2 Play the Inversion Patterns in C, D, E, F, G, and A.

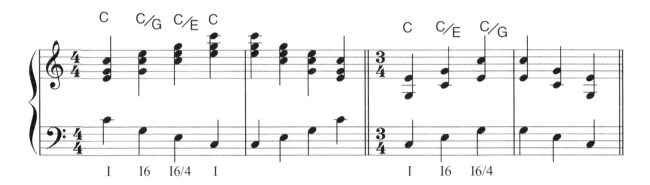

The RH in measures 1&2 has closed voicings, whereas measures 3&4 has open voicings. See the explanation of open and closed immediately below.

Closed and Open Voicings

In closed voicing, the notes are tightly positioned as possible. *In open voicing*, there are gaps between the soprano and alto, or alto and tenor.

Example 5.3 Closed Spacings Up the Octave. Play in C, D, E, F, G, and A.

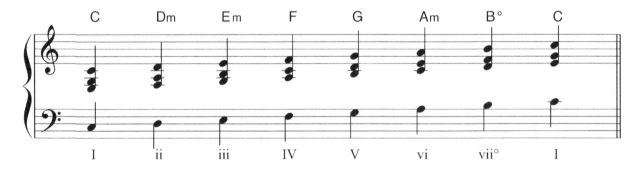

Below, let's apply open spacings to the major scale. Notice the series of 10th between the bass and soprano.

Note particularly the open C/E and F chords. The RH C/E chord is open: it does not have the full triad in the RH. Similarly, the RH F chord is open: it lacks the full triad in the RH.

Example 5.4 Open Spacings Up the Octave. Play in Keys of C, D, E, F, G, A.

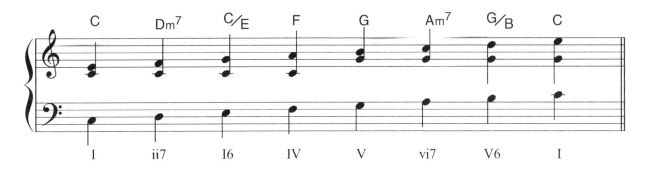

Notice the above spacings fall comfortably for your hand (important when improvising!).

Moreover, the ii7, I6, vi7, and V6 chords are often substituted for the ii, iii, vi, and the vii chords respectively. The vii diminished triad is rarely used in root position. When the melody is stepwise, 10ths between the bass and soprano work well (as above and below).

The same spacings are applied below.

Example 5.5 *Joyful, Joyful* (Play in Keys of D, E, F)

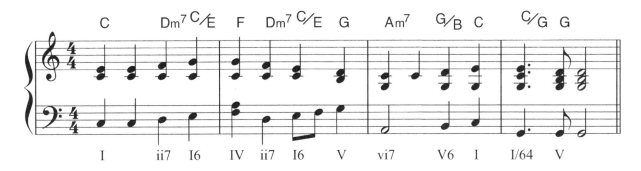

Try it! Pay special attention to Roman Numerals. Let them guide you.

For a bigger sound, use octaves in the right hand, and drop the bass an octave (as below).

Example 5.6   Same Material, But Bigger Sound

For more on different kinds of spacings, like 3+1 and 4+2, see chapter 11. If the above was difficult, take heart—the progressions below are easier!

Pachelbel Cannon (Down a 4ᵗʰ)

The famous "Pachelbel Cannon", which features progressions down a 4ᵗʰ, conveys a powerful sense of forward movement. As you work on these excerpts in various keys, focus your ear particularly on the *bass* part.

Anticipate aurally — listen. Where the chords are going? This is an important first step in learning how to improvise (without notated music) any song someone asks you to play. When you can play the progressions tolerably well, practice in the various keys *with your eyes closed or the book closed!* This will help develop your ear.

Example 5.7 Progressions Down a 4ᵗʰ. Play in C, D, E, F, G and A.

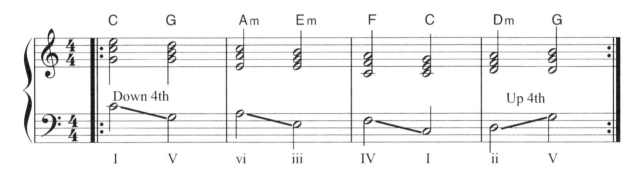

(One chord deviates from Pachebel's Cannon: a ii chord (m. 4) is inserted in place of his IV chord.)

Try it! Once you can play the progression, try your hand at embellishing it. Variations are available on the Internet to stimulate your imagination.

Now let's see how this series works out in a well-known worship song, *Give Thanks*.

Example 5.8 *Give Thanks* (Play in C, Bb, A, G)

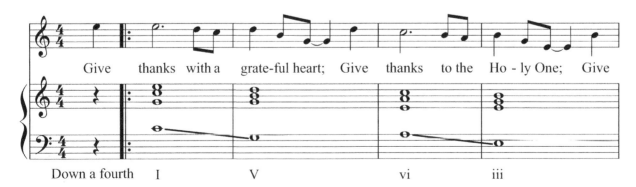

Try it! Play it in different keys. Improvise upon it. Call out the Roman Numerals, the Pop Symbols, or sing along.

Camouflaged Descending 4th Pattern.
Below, look at the descending, stepwise chord pattern. The descending 4th Pachebel progression remains, but is camouflaged. The 2nd, 4th, and 6th chords are now in first inversion (see asterisk). For example, the former G chord becomes G/B. And first inversion chords alternate with root position chords (eg., G/B → Am). You will find many opportunities to use this step-wise bass pattern in hymns and praise choruses.

Example 5.9 Step-wise Descending Pattern Through the Octave
            (* indicates 1st inversion chord) Play in keys of C, Bb, A.

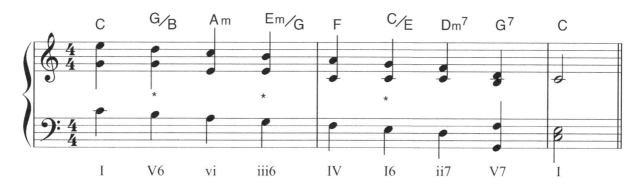

Example 5.10 *Give Thanks* (Pattern Above Applied) (Play in C, Bb, A)

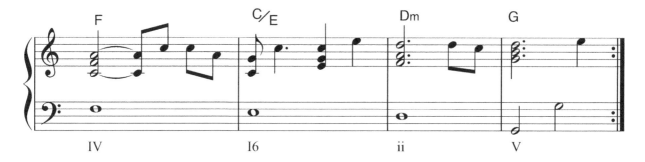

Try it! Also try chording and singing simultaneously (play no melody).

Example 5.11 Octave Doubling (* indicates a first inversion chord)

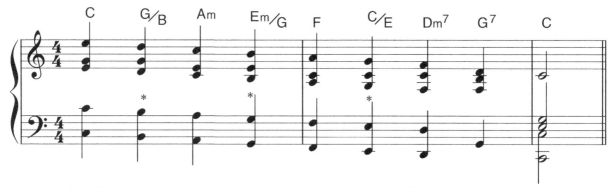

Let's apply this stepwise pattern, a harmonic alternative, to *Give Thanks*.

Example 5.12 *Give Thanks* (Octave Doubling) Play in C, D, E, and F.

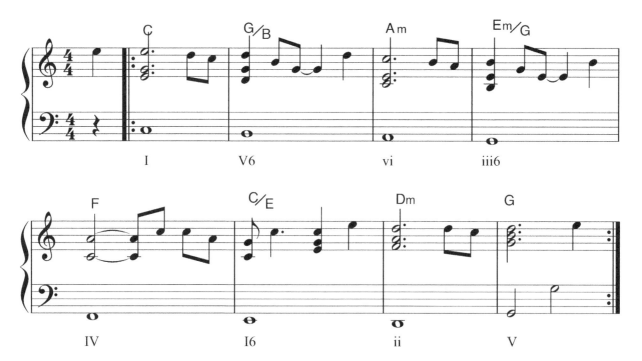

Principle. When choosing voicings, choose those that fall easily for your hand. Notice, the F chord (m. 5) doesn't continue the RH octave doubling (the low A below middle C).

Why? The major sixth (C to A) in the RH results in a more comfortable hand position to play the melody notes in beats 3 and 4. *There's no necessity to be rigid in your use of octaves!* Again, use the voicings that fall most comfortably for your hand.

Example 5.13 *Jesus, Name Above All Names* (Octave Doubling). Play/Sing in C, E, F.

Simple Triads Can Be Evocative. *Revelation Song* (Jennie Riddle) has a sacred, mysterious, other worldly atmosphere. Can we capture/unlock that atmosphere by means of sound? Can we "text paint" that feeling? Compare these two versions.

Example 5.14 Triads in Close Position (Revelation Song)

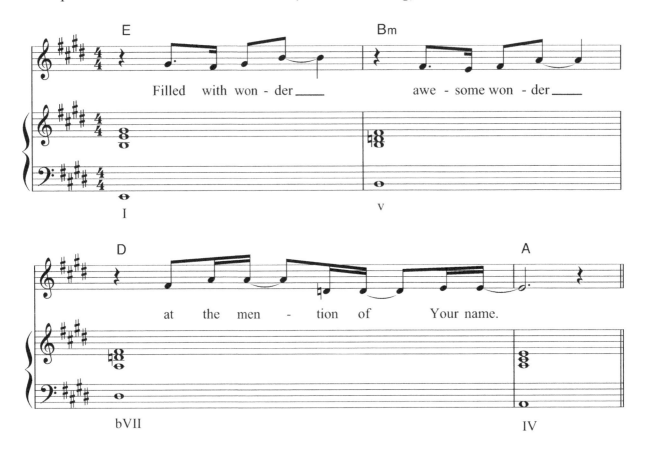

The spacing below keeps the third of the chord in the soprano. Tenths are sustained between the bass and the soprano.

Example 5.15 Triads in Open Position *(Revelation Song)*

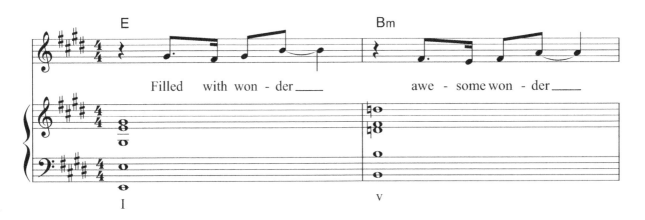

Quite a difference! It shows that intrinsic power can reside in an ideal spacing. The B minor chord is particularly effective. The open spacing and the lurching feeling of the chords winging across an expansive pitch space helps project a sense of mystery, wonder. Clearly, the sensitive use of voicings can lead to "text painting," one of our major goals.

Progressions Down a 5th, Up a 4th

Example 5.16 Progressions Down a 5th (Chorus of *Give Thanks*)

At the end of the chapter, see a chart for practicing progressions down a 5th and up a 4th. Progressions down a 5th are common; they have a strong forward movement, harmonically. They are "big" in Jazz and are really useful in hymns and choruses.

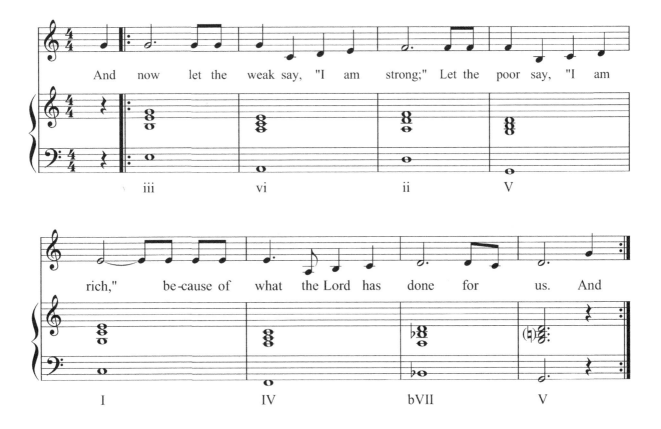

Try it! Let the Roman Numerals guide you. Call out the Roman Numerals. The chords above could be more smoothly connected (e.g., by retaining the G in the soprano for the second chord). However, I've discovered that this presentation is easiest for students new to improvisation. The next chapter will connect the chords more smoothly.

Example 5.17 *Give Thanks* (Verse in Descending 4ths; Chorus in Descending 5ths)

Playing the bVII chord. *F*or the bVII chord in the Chorus (below), go to scale degree 7, flat it a half step, and play a major chord. Also, play the Verse chords in root position.

Example 5.18 Play All of *Give Thanks* in C, Bb, A, G, F. Sing along!

Verse.   Descending Step-wise Bass Part (Roman Numerals)

Give | thanks   with a | grateful heart, give | thanks   to the | Holy One, give

    I   V6   vi   iii6

|Thanks   because he's | given   Jesus | Christ   his | Son.   And |

IV   I6   ii   V

Chorus.   All chords are descending perfect 5ths with exception of last chord

| Now   let the | weak say "I am | strong, "   let the | poor say "I am

  iii   vi   ii   V

| rich" because of | what   the Lord has | done   for | us

I   IV   bVII   V

Example 5.19   *Spirit Song* (Play in C, D, E, F)

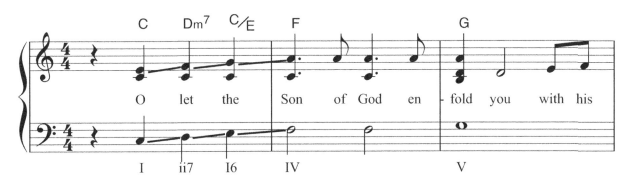

The two charts below are offered to help you do some "wood-shedding." Use them to solidify and gain mastery the shapes/inversions of major and minor chords in every key.

Practicing the Cycles

The charts below equip you learn the major and minor chords in *all* the keys. Learn them all! In his book, songs and song arrangements are limited to the "white" keys (C, D, E, F, G, A) in order to reduce the learning curve and to allow material to be covered quickly. However, when you learn these charts in the various ways suggested, you will be learning more than an isolated chord, you will be learning invaluable chord progressions and the process will help you begin to "think in music."

The spellings of chords are for ease of reading and performance, and do not always reflect the "correct" theoretical spelling. For example, a minor chord on Db (technically) consists of a lowered third (a minor third) above the root, that is, an F flat. For ease of performance an E is written below (a different spelling *but* the same sound results).

Example 5.20   Spelling a Db Minor Chord

Theoretically   Correct   Spelling   Ease   of   Performance   Spelling

Db Major   Db Minor   Db Major   Db Minor

Example 5.21   The Major Triad Through the Cycles (1, 3, 5 for each Scale)

C	C E G	E G C	G C E
F	F A C	A C F	C F A
Bb	Bb D F	D F Bb	F Bb D
Eb	Eb G Bb	G Bb Eb	Bb Eb G
Ab	Ab C Eb	C Eb Ab	Eb Ab C
Db	Db F Ab	F Ab Db	Ab Db F
F#	F# A# C#	A# C# F#	C# F# A#
B	B D# F#	D# F# B	F# B D#
E	E G# B	G# B E	B E G#
A	A C# E	C# E A	E A C#
D	D F# A	F# A D	A D F#
G	G B D	B D G	D G B
Bass	**Root Position**	**1st Inversion**	**2nd Inversion**

The chart is divided into groups of four for easy reading and performing. Consider practicing four rows or columns as a small group (initially) before attempting the entire cycle. Create a four row or column loop—repeating it until it is fluent.

Playing the Horizontal Rows (across the page)
1. Playing <u>up</u> the chart from the bottom row results in the descending fourth cycle (down a fourth = up a fifth).
2. Playing <u>down</u> the chart rows results in the descending fifth cycle (down a fifth = up a fourth)

In this book and the others in the series, the descending fifth cycle will be more strategic.

Playing the Vertical Columns
1. Play only the root position chords up and down the column
2. Play only the 1st inversion chords up and down the column.
3. Play only the 2nd inversion chords up and down the column.

Example 5.22 A Way to Play the Descending Fifth Rows (Across the Chart)

Another practice option is to go to the next closest inversion. For example, using the four chords above, and continuing, the following type of practice is even more practical.

Example 5.23 Going Horizontally to the Closest Inversion Results in I - IV Alternations.

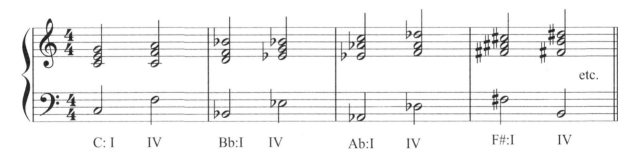

The same instructions apply to the minor triad (below).

Example 5.24 Minor Triad Through the Cycles (1, b3, 5 for each Scale)

C	C Eb G	Eb G C	G C Eb
F	F Ab C	Ab C F	C F Ab
Bb	Bb Db F	Db F Bb	F Bb Db
Eb	Eb Gb Bb	Gb Bb Eb	Bb Eb Gb

Bass	Root Position	1st Inversion	2nd Inversion
Ab	Ab B Eb	B Eb Ab	Eb Ab B
Db	Db E Ab	E Ab Db	Ab Db E
F#	F# A C#	A C# F#	C# F# A
B	B D F#	D F# B	F# B D
E	E G B	G B E	B E G
A	A C E	C E A	E A C
D	D F A	F A D	A D F
G	G Bb D	Bb D G	D G Bb

I wish to acknowledge Rique Pantoja and Jun Lee for devising/organizing/displaying the valuable "cycle charts" which appear in these volumes.

Talk to Yourself. In leading worship, we have the most amazing story to tell. However, Sundays are relentless. They keep coming! From time to time, we may find ourselves lacking energy, passion, or focus.   So…

**I sometimes talk to myself and prod myself this way
before leading worship**
If you don't feel anything, they won't either.
If you don't risk anything they won't either.

If your worship isn't costly,
theirs won't be either.

In the book of Revelation (ch5) the note of costliness is struck, indelibly,
through the image of a slain lamb:

*You are worthy to take the scroll and to open its seals,
because you were slain, and with your blood
You purchased men for God from every tribe
and language and people and nation.*
Rev 5:9-10

Major and Minor Seventh Voicings

- 17 pages
- 36 examples

OUTLINE	REPERTOIRE
Voicings for Major & Minor 7ths	Be Thou My Vision
Closed, Open, & Shell Voicings	When I Survey the Wondrous Cross
Practicing the Cycles	Spirit Song In Christ Alone
A Biblical Concept of Performance	Before the Throne of God Above

Seventh chords are a big deal! Seventh chords impart significant harmonic color. To highlight their coloristic features, open, closed, and shell voicings are discussed. Additionally, exercises are crafted to help you attain *command* of major and minor sevenths, so can use and have instant access to a variety of contrasting, nuanced, good-sounding spacings. With effort, by the end of this and the next chapter you should not only become familiar, but adept and proficient with a variety of seventh chord voicings.

Compare *Be Thou My Vision* without and with major and minor 7th chords.

Example 6.1 A/B Comparison of Major/Minor Triads Versus Major/Minor Sevenths

A. Use of Triads in *Be Thou My Vision*

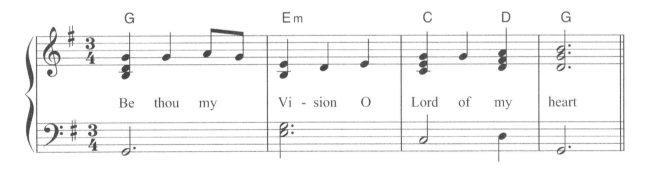

B. Use of Major and Minor Sevenths in *Be Thou My Vision (Warmer Version?)*

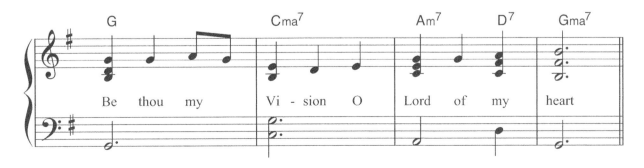

Does the creamy, mellifluous quality of the sevenths tend to warm up the piece harmonically?

Let's look at one more A/B comparison. Experience the difference. The sevenths in *When I Survey the Wondrous Cross* (tune: *The Water is Wide*) have a telling effect. In order to present a fair comparison, I have tried not to "stack the deck" in favor of the sevenths. Bass lines and inversions were created to ensure the triadic version had musical interest as well.

Example 6.2 A/B Comparison of Major/Minor Triads Versus Major/Minor Sevenths

A. Use of Only Triads in *When I Survey the Wondrous Cross*

B. Use of Various Sevenths in *When I Survey the Wondrous Cross*

True, sus chords and sevenths with raised fifths were also included, but major and minor sevenths contributed greatly to the aesthetic effect. We desire worship is to express our souls—"soul worship" to God. Sevenths can be one means of moving in that direction.

Voicings for Major & Minor 7ths

Become adept with various voicings. Memorize and absorb the tactile feeling of them in your hands. The ability to have "command" of an assortment of voicings is essential if we are to take full advantage of the range of harmonic colors inherent in major and minor sevenths and other sonorities in these volumes.

Seek to be able to voice a seventh, instantly, several different ways. Different voicings tend to project different meanings. It's a way to text paint. Some project power, others warmth, or the most delicate, nuanced feelings. Touch. Taste. Feel.

Example 6.3 Major 7ths Rotated. Measure 2: the bass is not doubled in the RH.

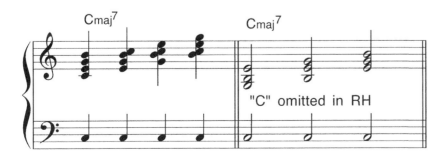

Example 6.4 Popular Major 7th Voicings in Root Position

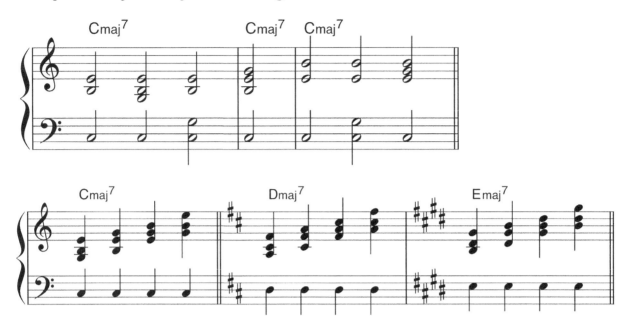

Example 6.5 For more Warmth Try Spacings With Open Fifths in the RH

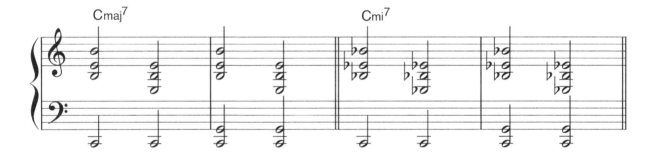

Example 6.6 Play the RH Inversions in C, D, E, F, and G.

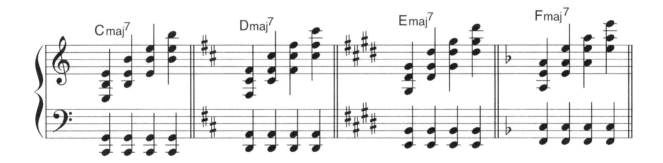

Below, let's immediately apply some of the above spacings.

Example 6.7 *Before the Throne of God Above*

Do you like the effect?

Example 6.8 ***Try it!*** Write In/Add and then Play the Major Sevenths *(In Christ Alone)*

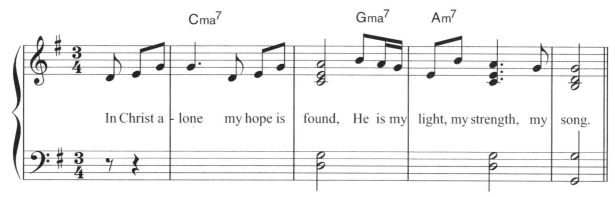

Example 6.9 Popular Inversions of Major 7th

Above, when the third, fifth, or seventh of the chord is in the bass (as above), it is often a good idea to omit that note from the RH. The result? — a cleaner sound. Also, the broken chord figure (B-C-G) is popular with the Cmaj/E chord in the RH.

Example 6.10 Cmaj7/E Illustrated in *Christ Alone* excerpt

Example 6.11 Dorian Scale Goes Well with Minor Sevenths

Above, did you notice that C→Eb→G→ Bb and D→F→A→C outline minor sevenths?

Example 6.12 Minor 7ths Rotated

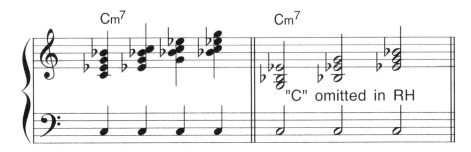

Example 6.13 Popular Minor 7th Voicings in Root Position

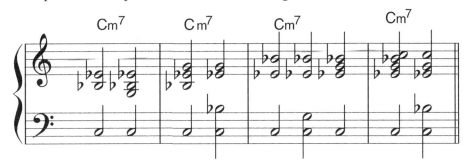

Example 6.14 Minor 7ths in Inversions

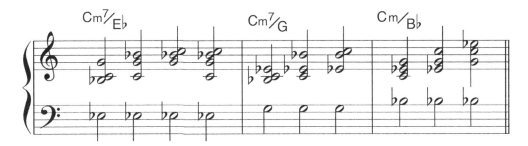

Again, if the third, fifth or seventh of the chord is in the bass, it's generally better to omit that note in the RH. This results in a cleaner sound.

Closed, Open, & Shell Voicings

See, below, three basic ways of spacing chords (closed, open, shell). Learn the chord patterns in all the keys. That effort will help you find your way around the different keys when you are playing a piece. If you do not know the major scale in all keys yet, learn that first, then proceed to the chords.

In closed voicing, notes are tightly positioned as possible. *In open voicing*, gaps occur between the soprano and alto, alto and tenor.

Example 6.15 Closed Spacings Up the Octave. Play in All Keys.

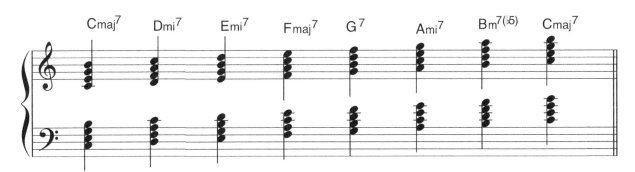

Now let's apply the above spacings to the major scale, with the third of the chord on top.

Example 6.16 Closed Spacings Up the Octave

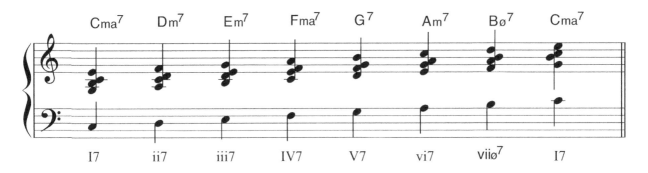

Example 6.17 Open Spacings Up the Octave. Play in All Keys.

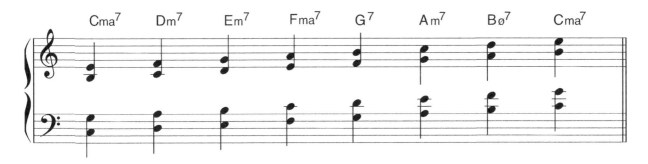

In shell voicing, only the *essential* notes of the chord are retained: below, the third and seventh are retained, but the fifth is omitted.

Example 6.18 Shell Spacings Up the Octave (no fifth). Play in All Keys.

Example 6.19 *Spirit Song* (Shell Voicing) Play it in Keys of C, D, E, F.

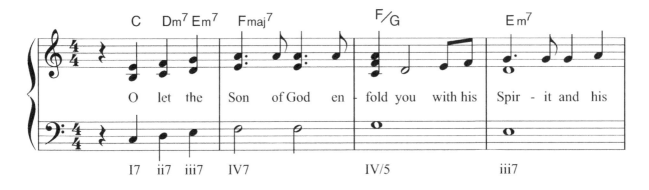

Try it! First, play the above example using the chords only (omit the melody) and call out the Roman Numerals (easiest!). Then sing the melody with the basic chords (more difficult). Finally, play the melody and the chords.

Example 6.20 Open Spacings Up the Octave (a warmer sound results). All Keys.

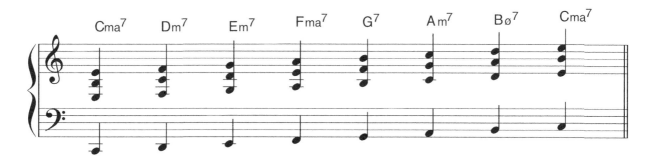

Example 6.21 In Higher Registers, More Doublings Can Occur. All Keys.

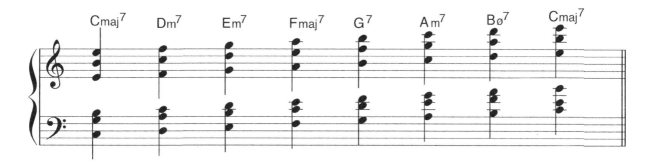

Another option. Drop the melody and obtain smoother chord connections (below).

Example 6.22 *Spirit Song* with Smoother Chord Connections (Play in C, D, E, F).

For the iii - vi - ii - V- I progression, notice the shell voicings. The inner voice alternates the *third* and the *seventh* of the chord, but there is no fifth. This pattern often works well.

Try it! Close the book. Let the Roman Numerals guide you. Memorize the iii - vi- ii - V - I progression.

In the following example notice the unique doublings that work best in a high register.

Example 6.23 *Spirit Song*   Unique Doublings. Play in C, D, E, and F.

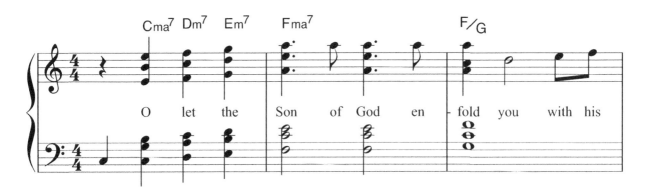

Spir - it and his | love. Let him | fill   your heart and | sat - is - fy your | soul.

iii7   vi7   ii7   V7   Imaj7

Further Options to Practice.

Example 6.24   Other Valuable Spacings applied to *Spirit Song* (Complete the Excerpt)

Try it! Play the entire piece applying the above voicings throughout.

The exercises below are intended to help us find major sevenths in all the keys (C, F, etc.). Each uses the series of descending fifths. *For further assistance in practicing the down a 5ᵗʰ, up a 4ᵗʰ cycle, see the chart at the end of the chapter.*

Example 6.25 Major Seventh Cycle (Down 5th, Up 4th). No Doubling.

Example 6.26 Major Seventh Cycle (Down 5th, Up 4th). Doubling.

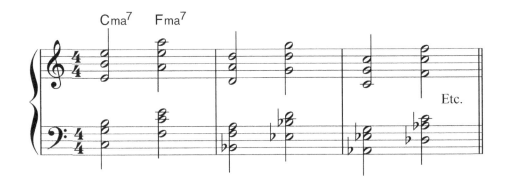

The following example is interesting in that a common tone is retained in the soprano part. You will find uses for this pattern! In fact it worked in measure one of *When I Survey the Wondrous Cross* (Example 6.2B)

Example 6.27 Major Seventh Cycle (Down 5th, Up 4th). Doubling.

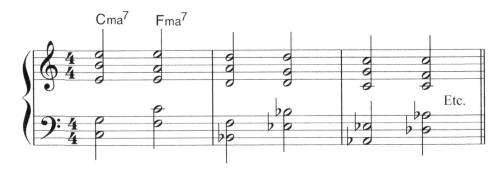

Notice below, the first two chords of 6.28 and 6.29 employ the same voicing relationship as 6.27 (Cmaj7 to Fmaj7) with the soprano note held.

Example 6.28 *Great is Thy Faithfulness* (Focus on Measure One)

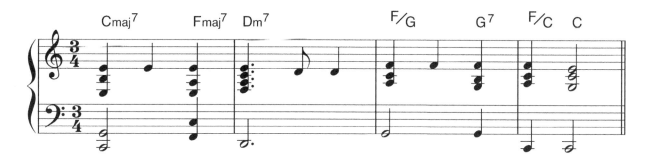

Example 6.29 *Joyful Joyful We Adore Thee* (Major & Minor Seventh Doublings)

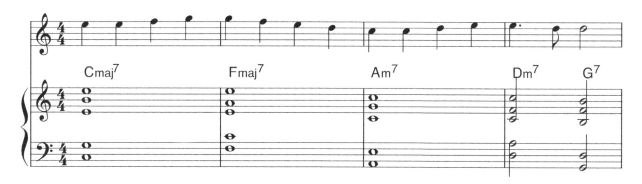

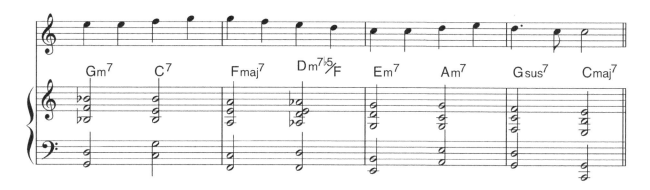

Example 6.30 Minor Seventh Cycle (Down 5th, Up 4th)

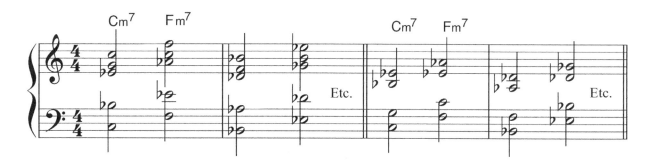

Example 6.31   Shell Voicings (ms. 1, 2, 5, 6, 10, 11, 12) in *Great is Thy Faithfulness*

Notice the 10ths between the bass and soprano. The texture is rather thin. If octaves are employed in the RH, the effect is much fuller and richer (as below).

Example 6.32 Octaves in RH (*Great is Thy Faithfulness*)

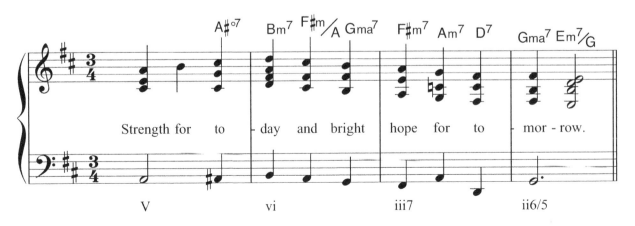

Practicing the Cycles

Example 6.33 Major Seventh Through the Cycle (3, 5, 7 of the Major Scale)

C	E G B	G B E	B E G
F	A C E	C E A	E A C
Bb	D F A	F A D	A D F
Eb	G Bb D	Bb D G	D G Bb
Ab	C Eb G	Eb G C	G C Eb
Db	F Ab C	Ab C F	C F Ab
F#	A# C# F	C# F A#	F A# C#
B	D# F# A#	F# A# D#	A# D# F#
E	G# B D#	B D# G#	D# G# B
A	C# E G#	E G# C#	G# C# E
D	F# A C#	A C# F#	C# F# A
G	B D F#	D F# B	F# B D
Bass	**Root Position**	**1st Inversion**	**2nd Inversion**

The chart is divided into groups of four rows for easy reading. You may also want to practice four rows as a group (initially) before attempting to play the entire cycle.

Playing the Horizontal Rows (across the page)
1. Playing <u>up</u> the chart from the bottom row results in the descending fourth cycle (down a fourth = up a fifth).
2. Playing <u>down</u> the chart rows results in the descending fifth cycle (down a fifth = up a fourth)
In this book and the others in the series, the *descending fifth* cycle will be more strategic.

Playing the Vertical Columns
1. Play the root position chords first.
2. Play the 1st inversion chords second.
3. Play the 2nd inversion chords third.

Example 6.34 One Way to Play Major-Seventh Descending Fifths (Across the Chart)

The most important thing to note is that the root notes (C, F Bb, Eb) are not played in the RH. That is, *the root is not doubled.* This is often a good voicing idea for major and minor sevenths.

Another practice option is to go to the next closest inversion. For example, using the four chords above, and continuing, the following type of practice is even more practical.

Example 6.35 Going Horizontally to the Closest Inversion Results in I - IV Alternations

The same instructions apply to the minor sevenths below.

Example 6.36 Minor Seventh Chord Through the Cycles (b3, 5, b7 of the Major Scale)

C	Eb G Bb	G Bb Eb	Bb Eb G
F	Ab C Eb	C Eb Ab	Eb Ab C
Bb	Db F Ab	F Ab Db	Ab Db F
Eb	Gb Bb Db	Bb Db Gb	Db G Bb
Ab	B Eb Gb	Eb Gb B	Gb B Eb
Db	E Ab B	Ab B E	B E Ab
F#	A C# E	C# E A	E A C#
B	D F# A	F# A D	A D F#
E	G B D	B D G	D G B
A	C E G	E G C	G C E
D	F A C	A C F	C F A
G	Bb D F	D F Bb	F Bb D
Bass	**Root Position**	**1ˢᵗ Inversion**	**2ⁿᵈ Inversion**

A Biblical Concept of Performance

In the definition below, the biblical emphasis on "scrving" and "ministering" (words used in the Old Testament relative to music making) can help alleviate the negative connotations often associated in churches with the word "performance." Generally, the people don't want to think of worship as a performance or "show." Understandable.

Yet for us musicians, the word performance is a central to our vocabulary and to our identity. We *are* performers, and we talk about ways to improve performance incessantly.

The biblical emphasis, fortunately, can help reduce "noise" in the church communication system, and also orient us spiritually in the right direction. For example, consider using language like this during a church announcement: "In the Christmas Pageant tonight, the Worship Band and Choir will perform, minister, and serve for the glory of God." Doesn't that establish a wholesome perspective?

A Biblical Concept of Performance
To perform is to do something complicated or difficult
with skill in public
with a view toward serving and ministering.

Major and Minor Seventh Applications

- 12 pages
- 23 examples

OUTLINE	REPERTOIRE
Progressions Down a 5th using 7th Chords	Give Thanks Be Thou My Vision
Give Thanks Possibilities	Great is Thy Faithfulness Spirit Song
Parallel Tenths Between Soprano and Bass	Before the Throne of God In Christ Alone
Drop 2 Voicing	Emmanuel Joyful, Joyful Seek Ye First
	Jesus, Name Above All Names

Sevenths are attractive! Sevenths function wonderfully in a variety of musical contexts: (1) in progressions descending a fifth, (2) in passages using parallel 10ths, (3) in melodic sequences, (4) in passages alternating sevenths and added second chords, (5) and with Drop 2 voicings. Learn, hear, and feel how they glide and connect. Apply them yourself in selected passages.

Progressions Down a 5th with 7th Chords

You will probably find the version below of *Give Thanks*, now with 7th chords, more attractive than the simple triadic version of a previous chapter. Notice how smoothly the chords glide. Common tones between chords help create smooth chord connections.

Example 7.1 Progressions Down a 5th with 7th Chords *(Give Thanks)*

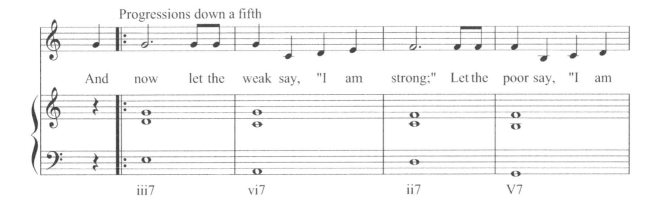

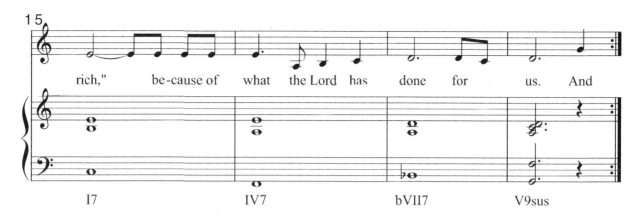

Common tones are retained in the soprano part (G in ms.1&2; F in ms. 3&4, etc.).

Give Thanks Possibilities

Now let's put the verse and chorus of *Give Thanks* together using 7th chords. In the verse we'll use three-note chords in the RH. In the chorus we'll use shell voicings in the RH. Once you can play it fluently, embroider your result with broken chords and melodic variations, especially on the chorus when the melody has long notes (dotted half notes).

Example 7.2 *Give Thanks*

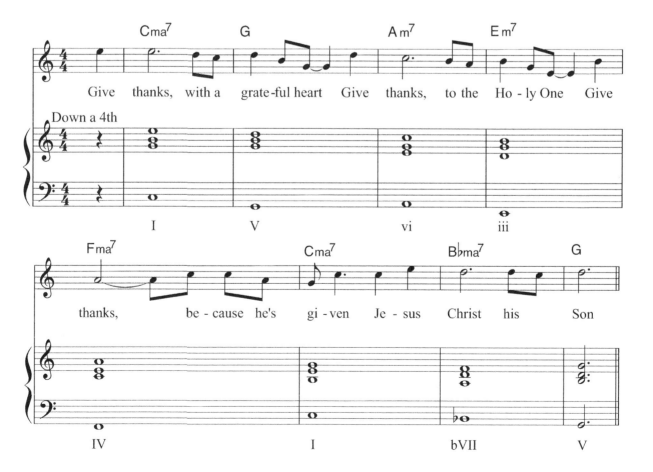

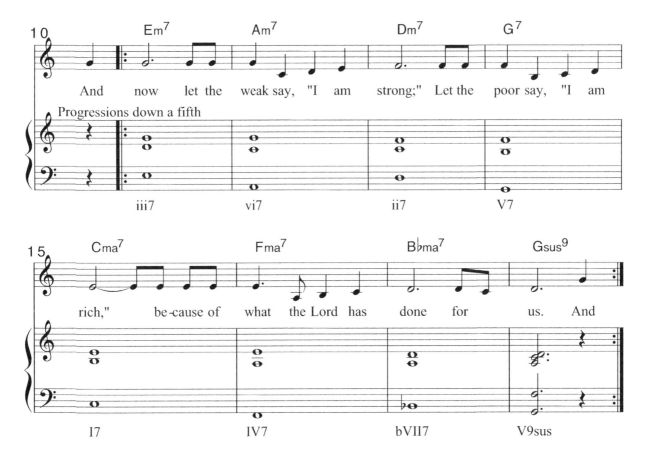

Melodic Sequences. Can you discern the melodic sequences in the RH?

Example 7.3   Alternative Two Note Melodic Sequence for *Give Thanks*

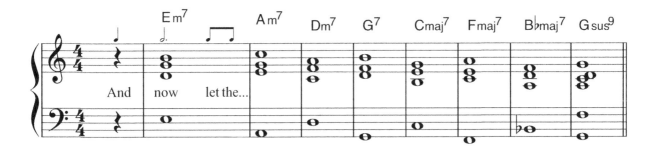

Try it! Improvise upon these chords. Also sing and play at the same time. Play it in the key of Bb, C, D, E. The melody of *Give Thanks* has a number of dotted half notes. *Embroider* those long notes.

Example 7.4   Another Two Note Melodic Sequence for *Give Thanks*

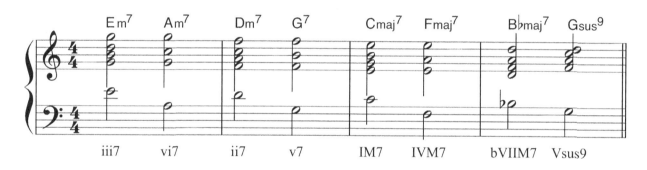

Try it! Improvise upon these chords. Also sing and play at the same time. Play it in the keys of C, D, E, and F. *Embroider* the dotted half notes.

Example 7.5 Yet Another Voicing Possibility for Chorus of *Give Thanks*

Descending 5ths with Octaves Doubled. Step-Wise Descending Soprano Line.

Try it! Improvise with the example above. Sing and play.

Example 7.6 Play All of *Give Thanks* in C, Bb, A, G, F. Sing along!

Verse (Several pairs of chords are descending 4ths)

Give | thanks   with a | grateful heart, give | thanks   to the | Holy One, give
    IM7   V   vi7   iii7

|Thanks   because he's | given Jesus | Christ   his | Son.   And |
IVM7   IM7   ii7   V

Chorus (All chords are descending 5ths with exception of last chord)

| Now   let the | weak say "I am | strong, "   let the | poor say "I am
 iii7   vi7   ii7   V7

| rich" because of | what   the Lord has | done   for | us
 IM7   IVM7   bVIIM7   V

Note: M7 means play a major seventh. Also, play the verse, alternating root position and first inversion chords so the bass part descends by step.

Added Second Chords. Added second chords create harmonic colors that students often find attractive.

Example 7.7 C Triad and C2 Chord Compared

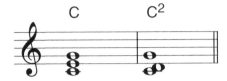

With a C2 chord (in the RH), the third of the chord is omitted and a second is added. We'll discuss them in detail in Book 2, but for now, let's get a little taste of them. Below, they are alternated with major and minor sevenths.

Example 7.8   Shell Voicings Combined with Added Second Chords
               (* indicates first inversion sound)

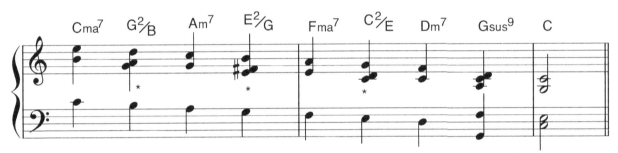

G2/B means: play a G2 in the RH; the note B in the LH. "B" creates the 1st inversion.

Example 7.9 Shell Voicings Alternative: *Give Thanks*

Bass part descends step-wise through the scale.

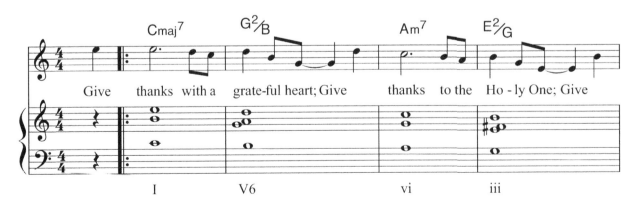

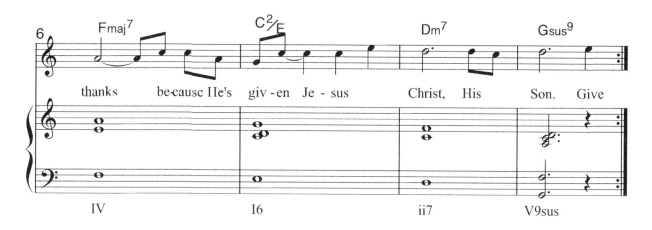

Parallel Tenths Between Soprano and Bass

Example 7.10 Step-Wise Octave Doubling *(Jesus, Name Above All Names)*

Bass part descends step-wise through the scale. Added seconds are integrated.

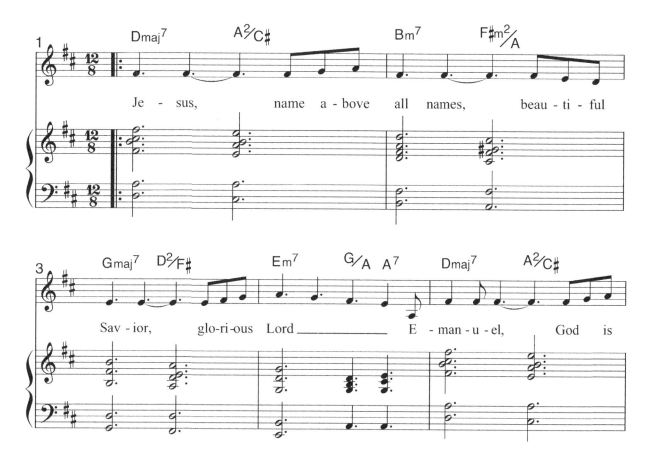

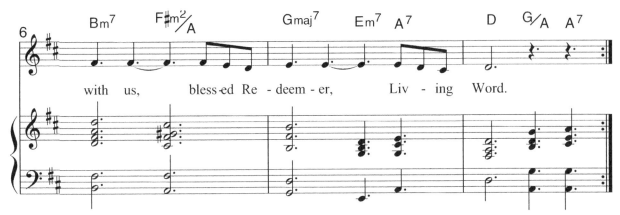

Notice above that several chords (A2/C#, F#m2/A, D2/A) function as passing chords.

Example 7.11 Step-Wise Octave Doubling *(Be Thou My Vision)*

Example 7.12 Octave Step-Wise Doubling *(Joyful, Joyful)*

Above, a few adjustments were made in ms 4 & 5 so the descending pattern would work.

Example 7.13 **Do it!** Create Step-wise Doubling. Write Pop Symbols for *Seek Ye First.*

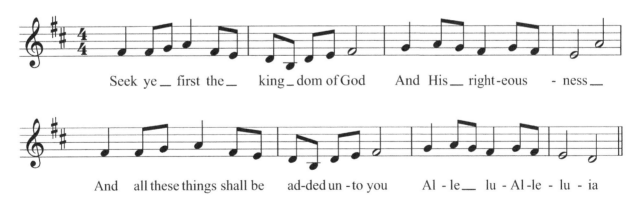

Exercises Writing Major and Minor Sevenths. Where appropriate, create major and minor sevenths for the following excerpts. Write the Pop Symbols above, and the exact voicings you consider best in the bass and treble clefs. Your chords do not need to follow the contour of the melody. Limit yourself to one or two chord changes per measure. Harmonize the entire passage.

Example 7.14 *In Christ Alone*

Example 7.15 *Jesus, the Very Thought of Thee*

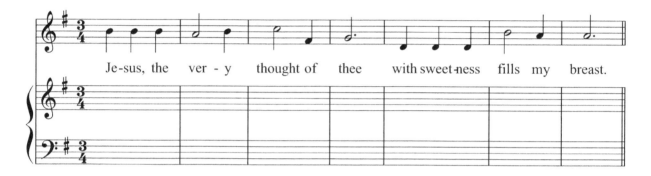

Example 7.16 *Savior Like a Shepherd Lead Us*

Drop 2 Voicing

"Drop 2 voicing" is a term/technique used by Jazz keyboardists. In drop 2 voicing, the second highest note in the close spacing of a chord drops an octave.

Example 7.17 Drop 2 Voicing

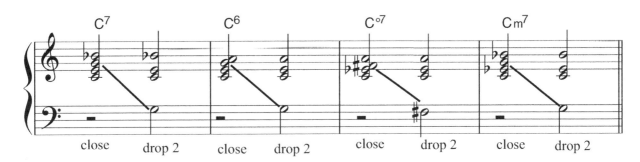

Guitarists often use this spacing. Chord inversions are handled the same way (as below).

Example 7.18 Drop 2 in the Inversions of a Major Seventh Chord

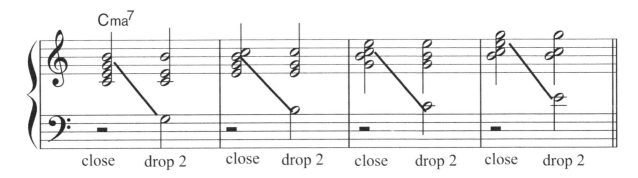

Example 7.19 Close Spacing in Right Hand *(Emmanuel)*

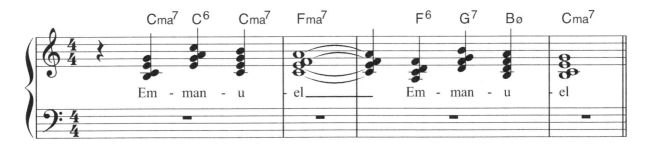

Example 7.20 Drop 2 Spacing Applied to *Emmanuel*

Possible Solutions to Previous Exercises

Example 7.21 *In Christ Alone*

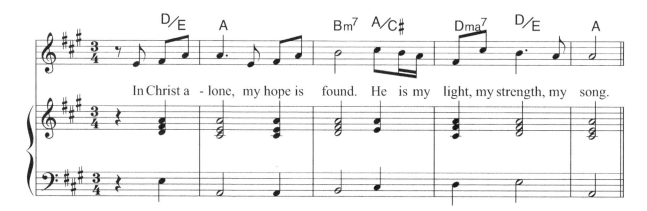

Example 7.22 Jesus the Very Thought of Thee

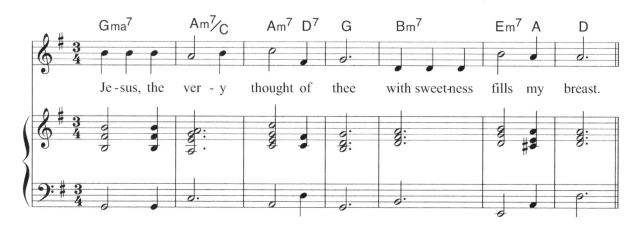

Example 7.23 *Savior Like a Shepherd Lead Us*

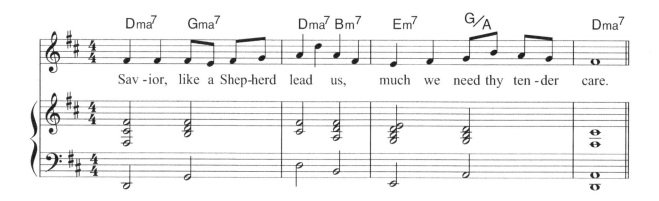

When to use major and minor sevenths? Smooth-sounding major and minor sevenths tend to warm up pieces harmonically. They are particularly effective in slower-tempo, expressive, tender, emotional pieces. Overused, they can become saccharine, like a too sweetened, sugary drink. Discernment is needed!

In contrast, straight triads and power chords (triads with no third) may be more fitting in assertive, angular, declarative, proclaimative, faster-tempo, militaristic pieces (like *Onward Christian Soldiers*).

Don't allow a perfectionist attitude to paralyze your progress.
You are going to make mistakes. Any improviser will make clams.
Perfect love casts out fear
I John 4:18

Nonetheless, seek to become skilled.
The words "skill", "skillful" and "skillfully"
appear 22 times in the building of the Tabernacle.
Here's a sampling of "skill" passages.

Moses called Bezalel and Oholiab
and every skillful one whom the Lord had given skill,
everyone who heart was stirred to come and do the work.
Ex 26:2

Kenaniah the head Levite was in charge of the singing…
because he was skillful at it.
I Chron 15:22

Sing to him a new song: play skillfully on the strings…
Ps 33:3

Do you see those who are skillful in their work?
They shall serve kings….
Prov 22:29

Alternating Harmonies (Doubles) I

> • 16 pages
> • 34 examples

OUTLINE	REPERTOIRE
Doubles—I-V Alternation	Amazing Grace Be Thou My Vision
Doubles—I-IV Alternation	Be Thou My Vision To God Be The Glory
Doubles— I-ii Alternation (Gospel)	The Solid Rock Holy Holy Holy
Doubles—I-dim7 Alternation	Come & Go with Me To My Father's House
Doubles—V-IV Alternation on Dominant	We've Come This Far By Faith
Doubles—i-VII Alternation	Lord, I lift Your Name on High
	O the Deep, Deep Love of Jesus

"Doubles" (alternating harmonies) are easy to employ. In this chapter we'll learn about the various ways they can function in a number of worship pieces.

Doubles are useful for embellishing a given chord, for creating more action and movement in an otherwise static music context, for creating harmonic color, enhancement, dissonance, tension, release, and harmonic syncopation. Doubles often function as energizers. Doubles occur frequently in Rock and Gospel Music.

What do we mean by " doubles" or " alternations"? How are we using these terms? A little background is needed. First, the concept of *passing* chords and *neighbor* chords.

Consider that in the harmonic context below, the RH notes C, E, G are chord tones, whereas the notes D and F are *passing tones* (PT).

Example 8.1 Passing Notes

In the same way, if a C chord remains the controlling sonority, the Dm chords below could function as *passing chords.*

Example 8.2 Passing Chords

Furthermore, do you agree that although the example proceeds up the scale, only two harmonies are alternated (C and Dm)? Two chords, a "double," are alternated. Doubles can function as *passing chords*.

Doubles can also function as upper neighbor (UN) or lower neighbor (LN) chords (as below). Observe: a C chord occurs (ms. 2, 3), then a UN or LN chord. Then C returns.

Example 8.3 Doubles Functioning as Neighbor Chords

Doubles are possible (especially) when the parent or given chord is long and allows sufficient time for an alternation to occur. The four-beat C chord allows ample time for an alternation to occur. Remember, doubles can function as passing or neighbor chords.

Terminologically, we distinguish an "alternation" from a "substitution." The C chord (above) is not *substituted* with another chord. It remains: it is not removed. Another chord does not take its place. Rather, the C chord is *alternated* with a Dm chord.

Finally, we can efficiently characterize the two examples above as a I → ii Roman Numeral alternation, a favorite stylistic element of Gospel Music.
Below, see a number of chords that are frequently used as doubles.

Example 8.4 Typical Alternations

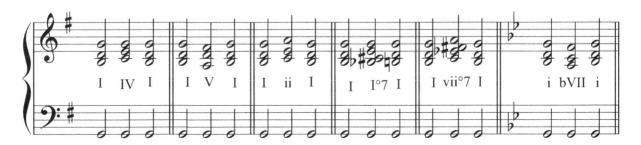

Remember, doubles can function as *passing* chords or *neighbor* chords.

Let's apply these "doubles" (alternative chords) to a fragment of *Amazing Grace.* You may like some alternations better than others. Which ones do you like best?

Example 8.5 Amazing *Grace*

The bVII chord functions better when embellishing a minor chord than a major chord. Thus the change to G minor.

Calculate the alternation from the root of the given chord. If we are performing a 1-IV-I alternation, as below (ms.1 &2)), we play the G chord (I) then the C chord (IV) and return to the G (I). The F chord (m.3) is the IV of a C chord.

Example 8.6 I-IV-I Alternation *(Amazing Grace)* Play it in G, F and E major.

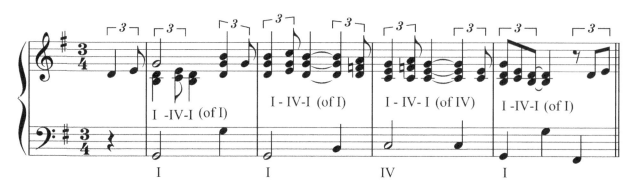

Try it! Play through the entirety of *Amazing Grace* using the I-IV-I alternation. Use the chart below.

Example 8.7 *Amazing Grace* (basic template)

Try it! Now play through the example above again using the I-ii-I pattern this time. You may have to make adjustments. Maintain a triplet feeling, and create some movement in the bass part. If this is too difficult for you, keep working through the chapter and come back to this assignment later.

Below, notice the alternating chords on the D chord (D-C-D) and C chord (C-G-C) below. They inject *movement* and *action* into the single harmonies.

Example 8.8 *Lord I Lift Your Name on High*

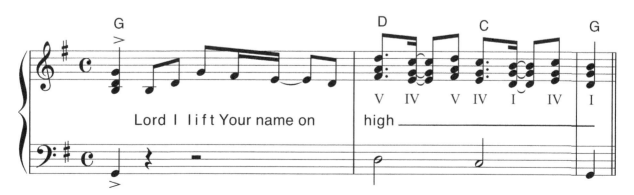

Doubles—I-V Alternation

"Doubles" (alternating harmonies) can be effective in both up-tempo songs and slow ballads—even hymns. As mentioned, it's a way to create harmonic movement. Below, look at the difference between passages with and without harmonic alternations.

Example 8.9 *The Solid Rock* without Alternations (static harmonically)

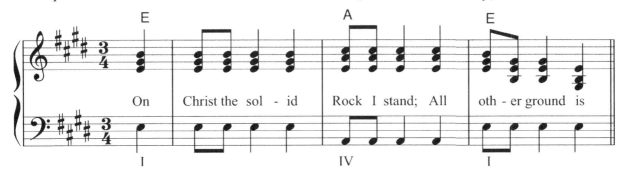

Example 8.10 The Solid Rock. V-I Variations (more dynamic harmonically)

Above, different variations are generated by varying the placement or rhythm of the V-I. Each successive example gives more weight to the V chord (B major). In the third presentation (the most dynamic version of the three), we are pulled more to the V chord. A harmonic shift took place.

Example 8.11 *The Solid Rock* with Syncopated Alternations (Yet More Dynamic)

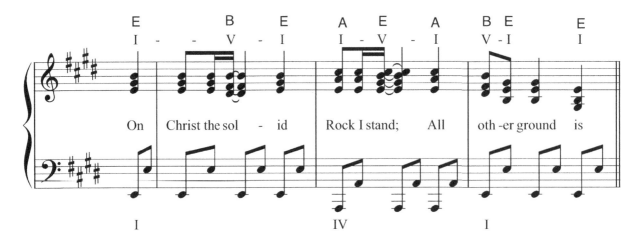

Experiment with the last two measures ("Rock I Stand; All other Ground"). Create some variations using the alternation idea.

The first three measures below express (abstractly) the basic harmonic relationships of the example above.

Example 8.12 The Basic I-V-I Relationships

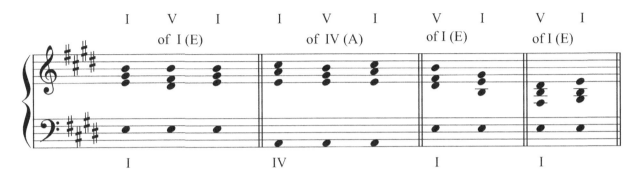

To establish the I-V firmly in our minds, let's play the progression (below) through the circle of fifths—E, A, D, G, C, F. Bb, Eb, Ab, Db, Gb, B, E. We begin with E major rather than C major because we want to learn "sharp keys" well. In these days when so much worship music is guitar led, sharp keys often get precedence.

Example 8.13   I-V through the Circle of Fourths (Up a 4th, Down a 5th)

The example below expresses (abstractly) that the I-V alternation can occur on scale degrees I, IV, and V. This means it can have a broader theater of application.

Example 8.14   I-V Alternation over I, IV, V

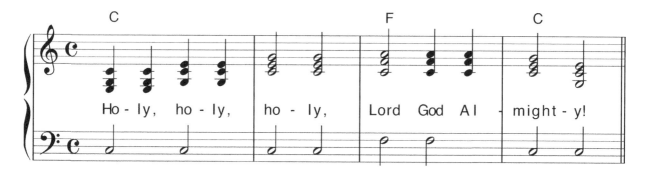

Doubles—I-IV Alternation

So far we have looked at the I-V alternation. We now take up I-IV alternation which also occurs frequently in Gospel Music. Doubles are a way to create motion over a single chord, as we will demonstrate in the examples below.

Example 8.15 *Holy Holy Holy* (*without* 1-IV-I alternation)

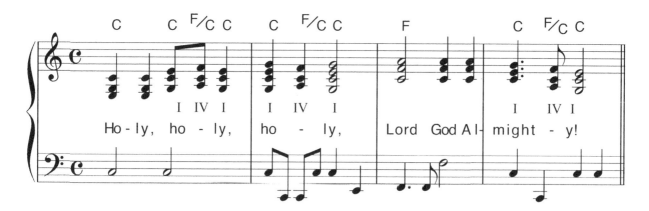

Example 8.16 *Holy Holy Holy* (with I-IV-I alternation)

The doubles in ms. 1&2 are neighbor chords, whereas m.4 is a passing-chord double. The doubles created more harmonic movement, and made the harmony less static.

Example 8.17   I-IV through Cycle of Fifths (Up a 4th, Down a 5th)
A.

B.

Try it! Create I-IV alternations with *Amazing Grace.*

Doubles—I-ii Alternation (Gospel)

A whole book could be devoted to Gospel/Blues techniques. However, in this and the next chapter we want to give you a peek at the how the I - ii - I pattern works in a Gospel environment. See two favorite African American songs written without much embellishment. I've seen black choirs process into the Church singing these songs!

The ii alternation below is so characteristic of much Gospel Music! Can you hear a choir singing the three-part RH chords? (By the way, instead of the ii chord, classical music would have substituted a V chord. That's one of the stylistic differences.)

Example 8.18 *Come and Go with Me to My Father's House* (I - ii - I)

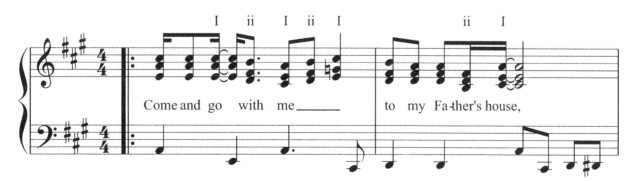

Example 8.19 *We've Come This Far By Faith* (I - ii - I)

Example 8.20 Exercise: I-ii-I Cycle of Fifths (Up a 4th, Down a 5th)

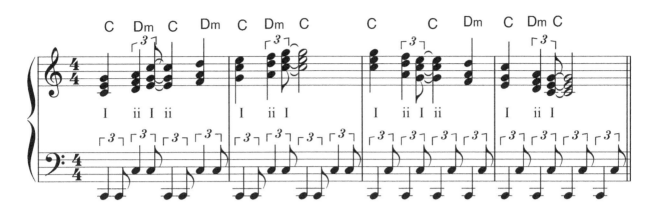

Play it! Play it in C, D, E, F, G, and A.

Example 8.21 **Try it!** Integrate the I-ii Pattern. *(I Must Tell Jesus)*

Doubles—I - dim7 Alternation

Example 8.22 I - dim7 - I through the Cycle of Fifths (Up a 4th, Down a 5th)

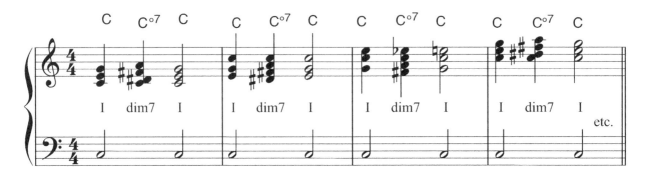

Example 8.23   Amazing Grace

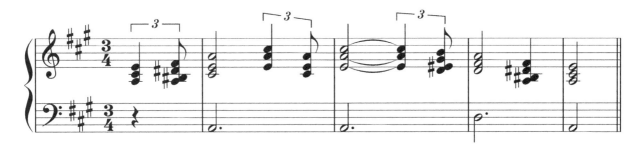

Try it! Improvise I -dim - I doubles with *Amazing Grace*. Use the chart below.

Example 8.24 Amazing Grace (Basic Chart)

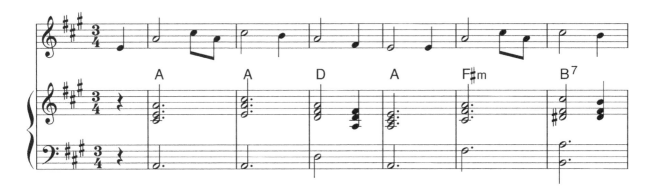

V - IV Alternation on the Dominant

Here's another easy chord alternation—alternation on the dominant (V). It can be used as preparatory step leading to half and full cadences, or as an enhancement. *Play the examples below in the keys of G, F, E, and D.* The IV/5 has been called a "hybrid" chord.

Example 8.25 IV/5 Leading to a Full Cadence (*Be Thou My Vision*)

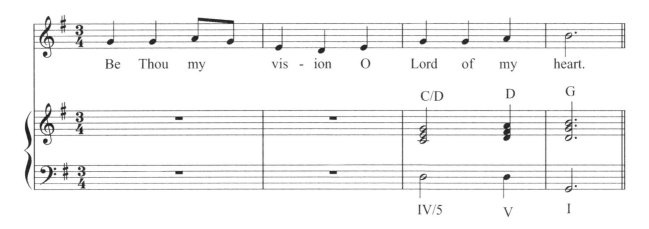

Example 8.26 IV/5 Leading to a Full Cadence (*To God Be The Glory*)

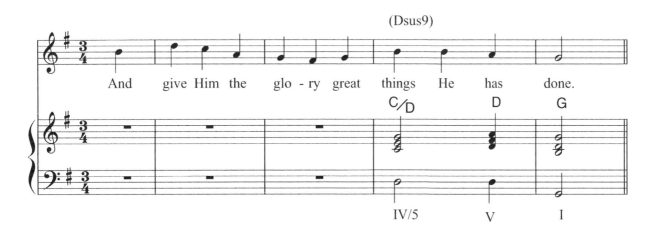

Note: when the melody is included in the analysis, a Dsus9 results.

Example 8.27 IV/5→V or V→ IV/5 Leading to a Full Cadence (*As the Deer*)

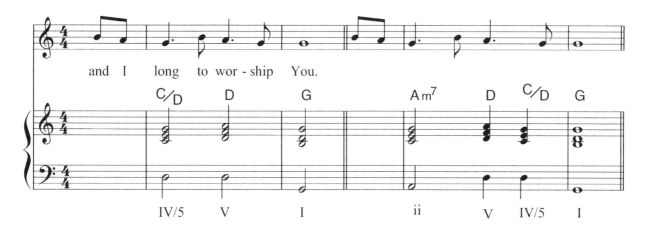

The IV/5 in the second example above acts as a harmonic enhancement.

Example 8.28 V→IV/5→V Movement in a Half Cadence (*Amazing Grace*)
A.

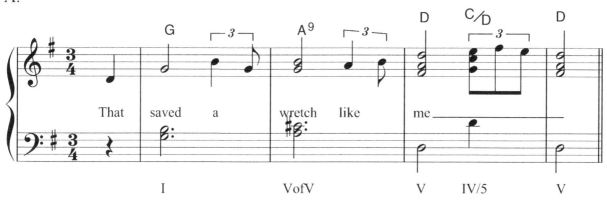

B.

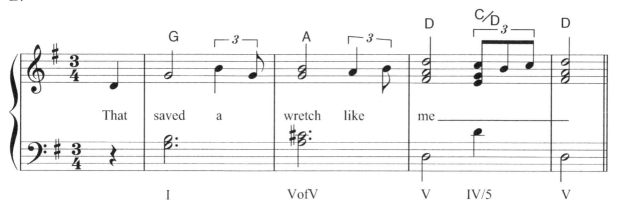

Above, the IV/5 chords act as neighbor chords.

Let's add some syncopation, and walk the bass up toward the I chord (D→E→F) to give the example more of a Gospel feel.

Example 8.29   Alternation at Half Cadence of *Amazing Grace* (Another Variation)

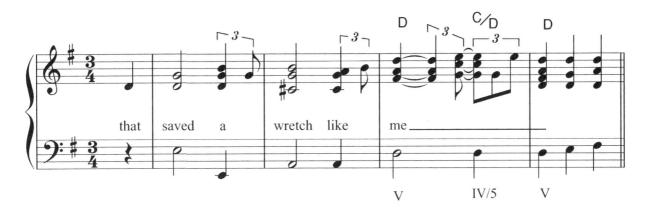

Now let's look at the relationship more abstractly.

Example 8.30   Dominant (V) in the key of G

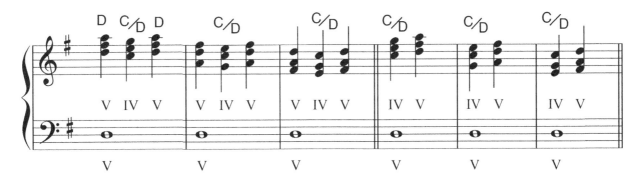

Try it! Play the example above in the keys of C, D, and E. Remember, the bass note should be scale degree five of the key of C, D, and E respectively. The IV-V alternation is also helpful in making modulations smoother and more secure (addressed in Book 4.)

Doubles—i - bVII Alternation

The i-bVII-i alternation occurs on scale degrees i and iv in minor keys and ii and vi in major keys. Also, a minor 11th chord results if all the thirds are retained.

Example 8.31   i - bVII over i and IV in Minor Keys

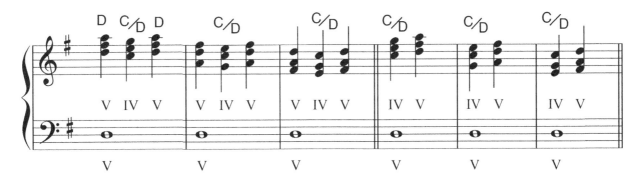

Below, the i-bVII relationship produces a gentle, rocking motion (like waves on the ocean) in this ballad-like piece. Note that the I-bVII occurs on scale degrees i and iv.

Example 8.32 i - bVII - i (*O the Deep, Deep Love of Jesus*)

In major keys the i-VII occurs most frequently on scale degrees ii and vi (as below).

Example 8.33 I - bVII - i in Major Keys

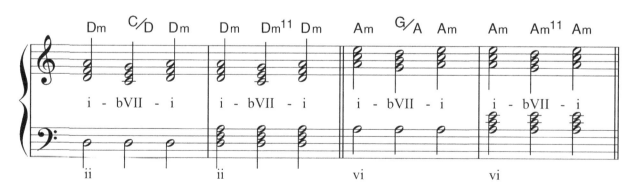

Example 8.34 Play i -bVII through the Cycle of Fifths (Up a Fourth, Down a 5th)

etc

Jesus
...a time is coming and now has come
when the true worshipers will worship the Father in
spirit and truth, for they are the kind of worshipers
the Father seeks. God is Spirit and his worshipers
must worship in spirit and truth.
John 4:23-24

Alternating Harmonies (Doubles) II

- 12 pages
- 22 examples

OUTLINE	REPERTOIRE
Doubles Applied to I, vi, IV, ii	Be Thou My Vision To God Be The Glory
Pedal Doubles	Come Into His Presence with Thanksgiving
Rock Doubles	Holy, Holy, Holy Every Move I Make
Gospel Doubles	Shout to the North and the South
Gospel Extensions	Amazing Grace Nothing But the Blood
Extensions to Added Seconds	This Little Light of Mine

Doubles Applied to I, vi, IV, ii

"Doubles" have to do with tension and release, dissonance and its resolution. When harmonies are too bland, doubles can create *more bite*. Moreover, they can be integrated into a wide array of basic chords including the I, vi, IV, and ii chords.

Example 9.1

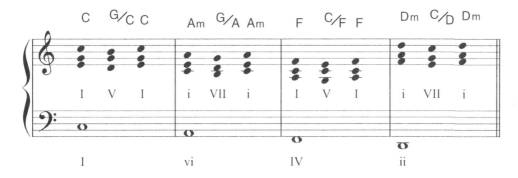

In the bass, a pedal occurs for each measure. In the treble, the Roman Numerals define how the alternating chord relates to the C, Am, F, and Dm sonorities. The alternating chord has an ornamental function—a lower neighbor function.

Try it! Play the above measures in the keys of C, D, E.

Below, see another variation of the above. A two rather than a three-chord pattern occurs. Every three-measure section reveals various right hand inversions that are possible. Also, note that in measures 4-6, the right hand remains the same as measures 1-3, while the left hand drops a third to A. This possibility makes creating variations incredibly easy. The same thing happens in measures 7-9 and 10-12.

Example 9.2

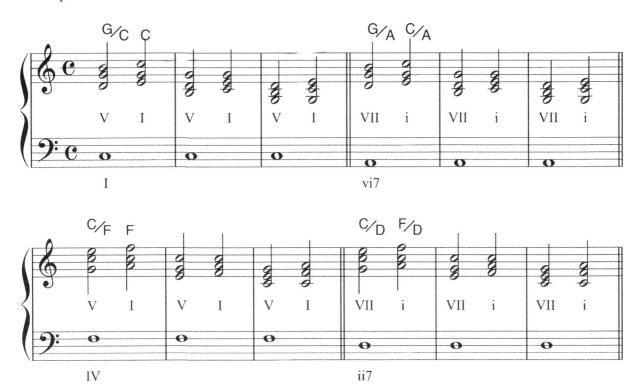

Explanation: for measures 4-6 and 10-12, the second chord is a minor seventh, a lower case one chord (i)—not a major chord—when the bass is considered the root.

Try it! Play the above two lines in the keys of C, D, and E.

Example 9.3 *Holy Holy Holy*

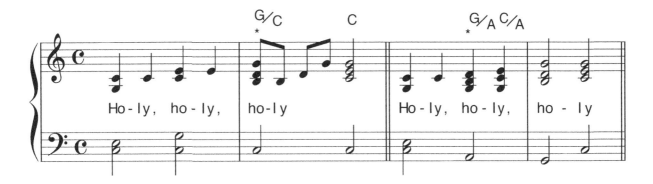

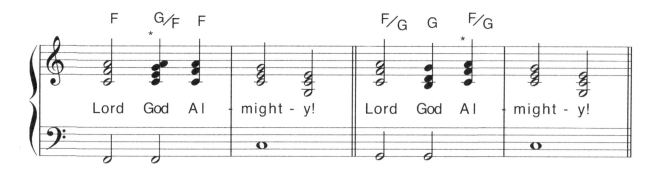

Did you notice the second chord in the second line (G/F) was slightly different from those earlier in the presentation? The soprano A was retained in the G/F chord. The result was more dissonant. A pedal on A occurred in the RH. Let's look at that now.

Pedal Doubles

Example 9.4 Pedal in Soprano Combined with Alternating Harmonies

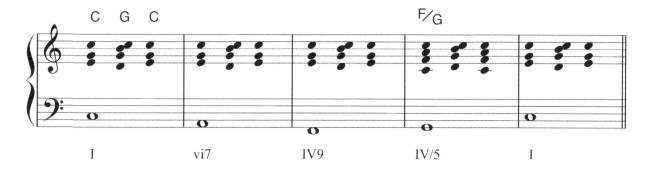

Do you like the effect?
Try it! Play the above example in the keys of C, D, and E.

Example 9.5 Hymnbook Version *(How Great Thou Art)*

Alternating rock harmonics are now applied (see the asterisked chords).

Example 9.6 Play it! Alternating Harmonies *(How Great Thou Art)*

Does this version sound more modern? Notice the first chord in measure three (C/F). Do you like the E-F clash in the right hand? The same thing occurs on beat four (C/D) in a D minor context. Sounds similar to these occur frequently in contemporary guitar music. **Try it!** Play the above example in the keys of C, D, and E.

Example 9.7 Typical Harmonies for *Shout to the North*

The harmonies below (I, IV, and V) are typically used in published versions.

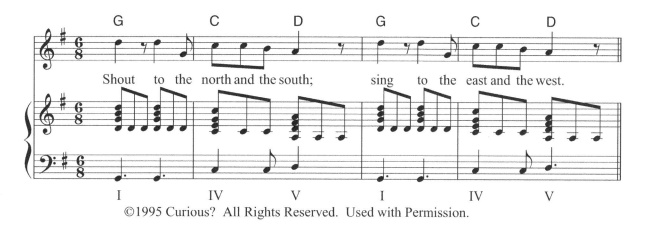

Example 9.8 **Improvise!** *(Shout to the North)*

Alternating rock harmonies are now applied (see asterisks). Play around (improvise) with the right hand. Try reversing the order of the alternating harmonies in each measure, for example. Maintain the bass part, however.

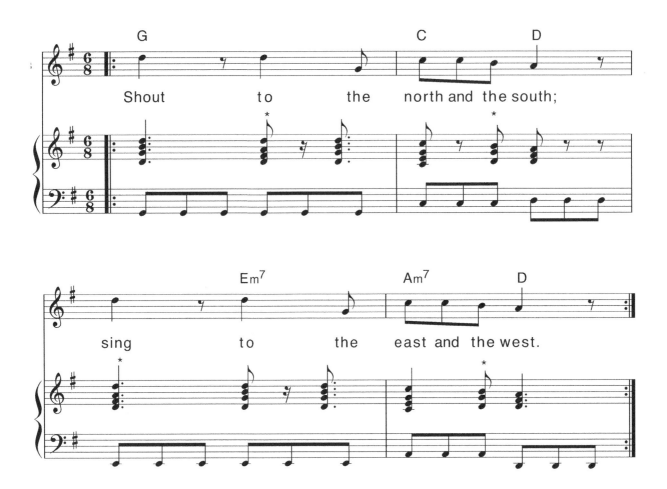

Example 9.9 Published Chords for *Every Move I Make*

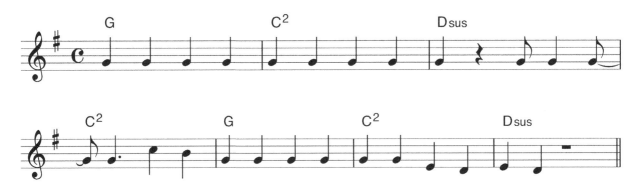

Example 9.10 **Improvise/Write** *(Every Move I Make)*

Create alternating rock harmonies. Label them and your pop symbols. Improvise various versions. A series of descending thirds is one chordal possibility.

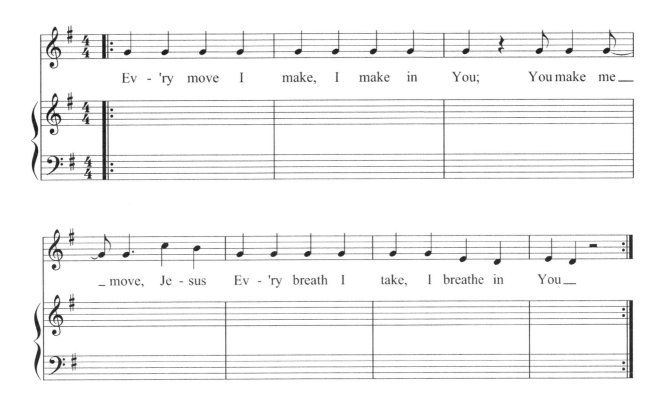

The alternating harmonies can also be applied to an up-tempo worship chorus.

Rock Doubles

Example 9.11   Hymnbook Version *(Come Into His Presence with Thanksgiving)*

We'll offer two rock versions. Notice the first two measures reveal a descending third relationship: the bass drops from C to A while the right hand chords remain the same.

Example 9.12 1st Rock Version *(Come into His Presence with Thanksgiving)*

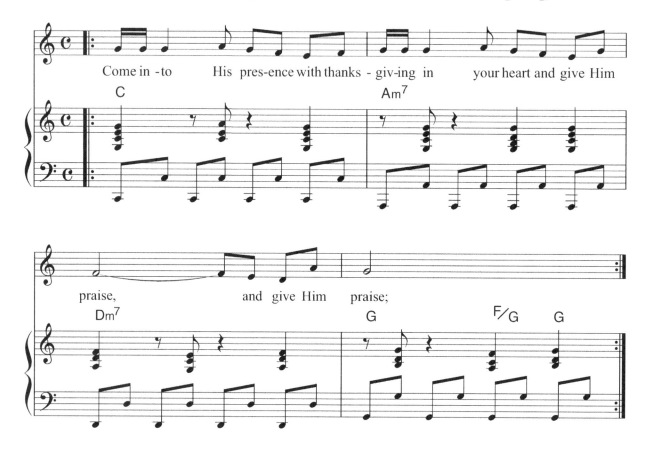

The chord progression contains the familiar series of descending fifths: I - vi - ii - V - I.

Example 9.13 2nd Rock Version *(Nothing But the Blood of Jesus)*

This version is harmonically the similar but with different rhythms and chord spacings.

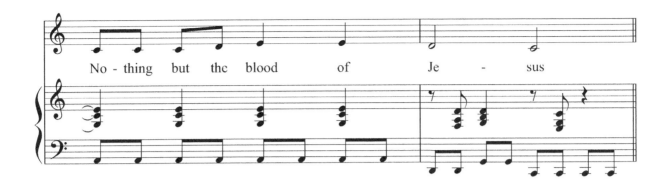

The asterisked chords (below) introduce a similar degree of tension into the texture.

Now, let's apply our alternating harmonies using Rock-like rhythms to the first phrase of *Be Thou My Vision*. Does this rhythmical treatment suit aura of the piece?

Example 9.14   *Be Thou My Vision*

In this case, I'm not sure the above rhythmic effect served the piece that well!

Gospel Doubles

Now furnish an entire version of the following two pieces.
You have six ways of alternating harmonies:
1. I-V   4. IV-V on the Dominant
2. I-IV   5. I - I°
3. I-ii   6. i -VII

These six options don't exhaust the possibilities, but they provide variety.
Write your alternation symbols into the lead sheet to help guide your improvisation.

Example 9.15 Project (*Amazing Grace*) Play along with the Track

Example 9.16 *This Little Light of Mine* (Gospel Style) Play along with the Track

Gospel Extensions

Example 9.17 Typical Gospel "Triple" Patterns

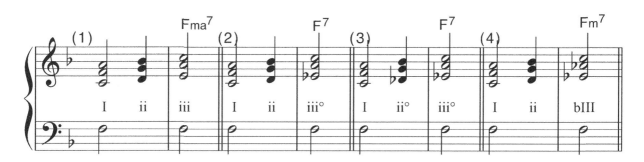

The Roman Numerals between the staffs apply to the three-note chords in the treble clef.

Example 9.18 Numbers (1) and (4) Employed in *Amazing Grace*

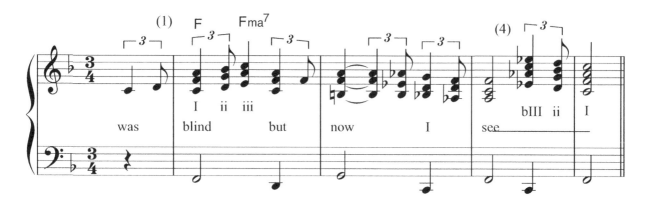

Note: (4) above, is particularly bluesy! The minor third movement (F to Ab to F) makes it unique. Could the example be effectively used as an introduction? Yes.

Example 9.19 A(bVII, IV, I) and B(bIII, bVII, IV, I) are Termed "Backtracking"

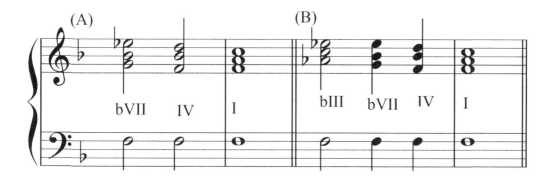

Instead of the pedal in the bass, the roots could (alternatively) be placed in the bass.

Example 9.20   bVII, IV, I Employed in *Amazing Grace*

Example 9.21 bIII, bVII, IV, I Employed in *Amazing Grace*

Extensions to Added Seconds

Alternating harmonies can be extended to include added second chords as well. We'll look at added seconds more in a later chapter, but here are some examples.

Example 9.22 Added Seconds Alternations on I, vi, IV, ii

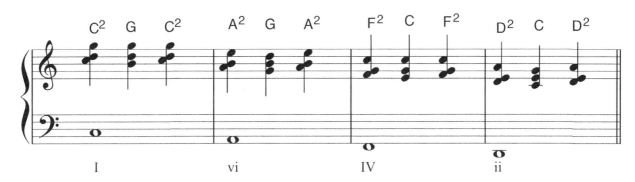

Do you have a need to be complimented?
Worship leading is a risky way to be built up.
Ministry tests your emotional maturity.

You don't believe me?
Read the book of Second Corinthians.
Even Paul faced very personal, stinging criticism.
Critics claimed his physical appearance wasn't
imposing, and his speaking delivery
left much to be desired.

*"His letters are weighty and forceful, but in person he is
unimpressive, and his speaking amounts to nothing."*
II Cor 10:10

Letting Go of the Melody/Arranging

- 18 pages
- 27 examples

OUTLINE	REPERTOIRE
Letting Go of the Melody	Amazing Grace
Chording	Be Thou My Vision
Scale Degree One	May the Mind of Christ My Savior
Scale Degree Five	Great is Thy Faithfulness
Try it!	Joyful, Joyful We Adore Thee
Exhaust the Possibilities	As the Deer
Summing-Up	Doxology
Riff Version	How Great is Our God

Letting Go of the Melody

Playing the melody takes energy and attention. Letting go of the melody is freeing. Letting go of the melody releases you to do other things, to text paint (get at the feeling of words), to explore alternative harmonies, to concentrate on melody and bass lines, to "orchestrate" the piece, to direct your energy into helping the people sing better. If the melody is unfamiliar or difficult and the congregation needs help, help them! If necessary, play it in octaves an octave higher so it cuts through. Also, if you are part of a band, your part needs to complement the other players.

This chapter has two main focuses: (1) processes for inspiring real-time worship and (2) processes for fashioning original arrangements. The two emphases are related.

Better progress is made if you work out 10 variations of a piece or passage than one or two variations of 10 pieces or passages. Why? Ten variations will force you to think, push yourself, stretch, and develop new material. By the end of this chapter you will appreciate more fully the logic and power of this statement.

In this chapter I will challenge you seriously! Consider letting go of the melody for a phrase or part of a stanza when leading a worship song. Some students have a hard time letting go of the melody. It's their crutch. The chapter will help you discover how to "let go" and experience the freedom of improvising in real time.

Chording

Imagine. You are part of a worship band. You are playing one of two ways: (1) playing a chord in the RH and a bass note in the LH; (2) only a chord in the right hand because you don't want to step on the bass player's notes. Perhaps you are playing an atmospheric pad with your RH on a synth. Let's look at the ways you could chord. Again, think of the examples two ways: as playing with both hands or only with your right hand.

In the following example the right hand doesn't play all the notes in the melody, but it does follow the basic contour of the melody. That's one option: follow the contour.

Example 10.1 Chart #1: Closely Follow the Melody with Your RH

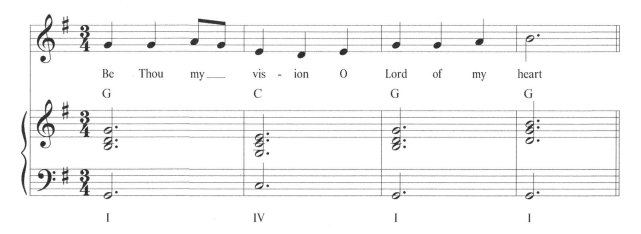

Example 10.2 Chart #2: Following the Melody Less

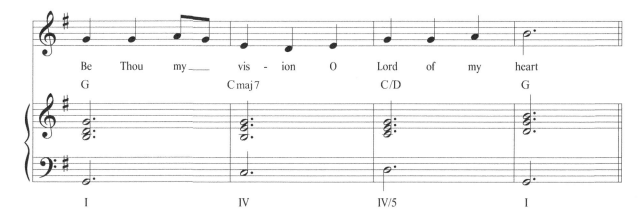

Example 10.3 Chart #3: RH Remains on Scale Degree 1 (G)

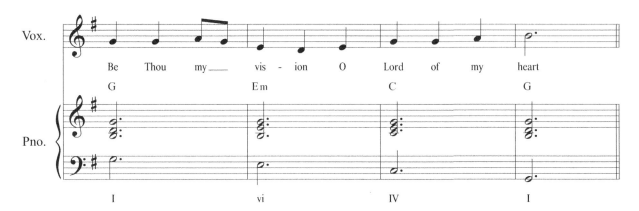

Consider this strange thing: limitations can spur creativity. Therefore, we are going limit ourselves. Our objective is to force ourselves to generate many new possibilities.

In chart #4 below, the soprano part is mostly limited to the note G (scale degree 1) but the harmonies are more adventuresome (that's the difference).

Example 10.4 Chart #4: More Complex Harmonies

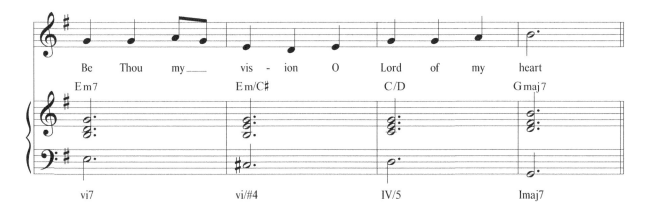

Do it! Create three harmonic variations. Keep the RH soprano part mostly on G.

Scale Degree One

When chording, one way to impose limitations is to maintain a single, centering note. Scale degrees one and five work best. Below, the soprano part remains (mostly) on scale degree 1.

Example 10.5 Be Thou My Vision

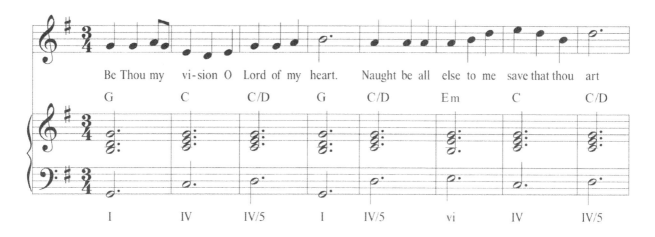

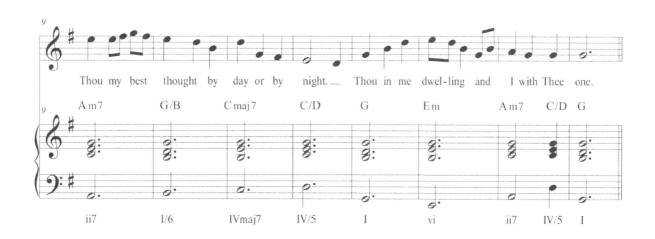

Notice the IV/5 chord at the half cadences (ms. 8,12) and full cadences (ms. 3,15). Observe the rising, step-wise bass line (ms. 9-12). Strong bass lines are critical in crafting quality progressions.

Example 10.6 Soprano Part Centered on the Scale Degree 1 *(Amazing Grace)*

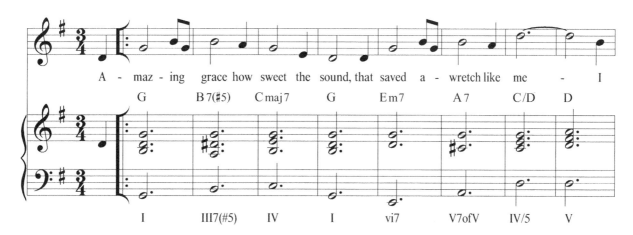

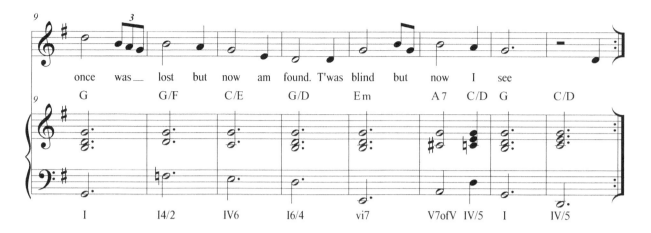

Try it! Experience the effect. Play it in the keys of G, F and A.

Below, a different harmonic variation occurs. This is *your turn* to create your own chord choices and center the soprano note (mostly) on G (scale degree 1).

Example 10.7 A Harmonic Exercise. Center the Soprano Mostly on G *(Amazing Grace)*.

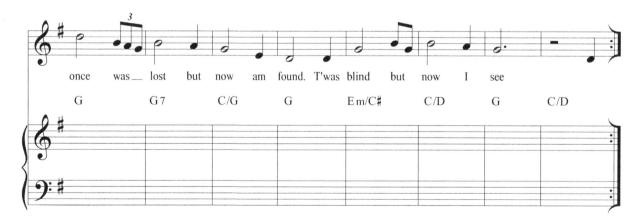

Did your result sound good? Any problems? For the Cmaj7 chord spacing (m.7), try G, E, B (top down). Play and sing the melody simultaneously in G.

Try it! Play in the keys of G, F, and E (possible keys for congregational singing).

Our next challenge is to create a Gospel feel ourselves. Study the stylistic elements in the first 8 measures below. Consider using some triplets in the LH or RH. Also try walking the bass up or down between notes. If you are experienced in writing music, write out the full notation (or jot some reminders). Otherwise, just improvise.

Example 10.8 Gospel Feel *(Amazing Grace excerpt)*

There's a lot of grit in the Gdim7/F# chord (m. 3). That happens in "black" stylings.

Playing Background Music. Centering in and around scale degree 1 or 5 is useful when playing background music while the pastor or someone else speaks. On the other hand, playing a known melody can be distracting. Why does one scale degree work better than another in a given piece? I don't know. In general, centering the soprano note on scale degrees 1 and 5 seems to work equally well.

Below, scale degree 5 is employed and the harmonization is more adventuresome.

Scale Degree Five

Example 10.9 Soprano Centered on Scale Degree 5 *(May the Mind)*

The following example is even more exploratory harmonically. For example, in the first three measures, the goal of the descending bass part is the ii chord on E.

Example 10.10   Soprano Centered on Scale Degree 5   *(Great is Thy Faithfulness)*

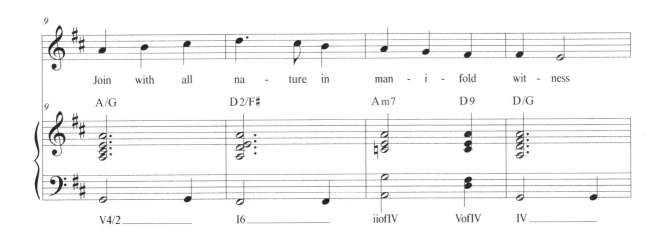

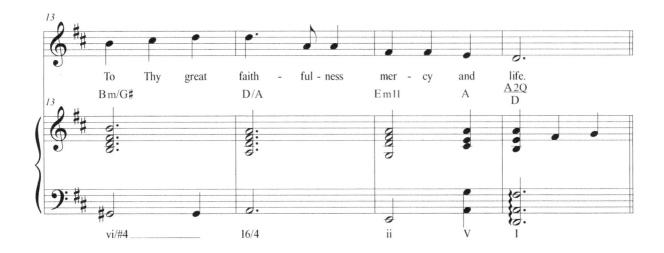

Again, when you are improvising pay attention to the bass part.
Crucial to effectiveness.

Try it!

Example 10.11 Center the Soprano on Scale Degree 5 *(Joyful, Joyful)*

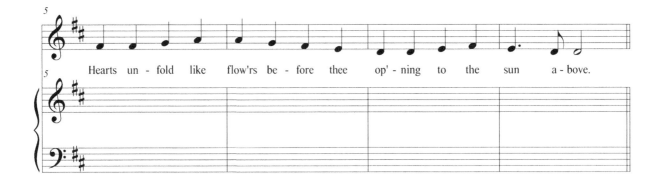

Example 10.12   Center on Scale Degree 1   *(As the Deer)*

Example 10.13   Center the Soprano on Scale Degree 1 *(Doxology)*

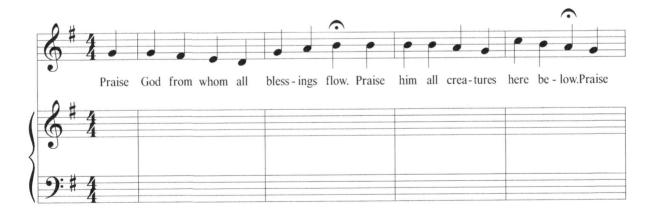

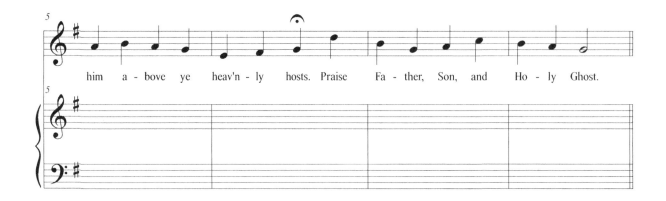

Exhaust the Possibilities

Suggestion. When you are trying to develop yourself…push yourself. Overwork a passage. Go crazy. You may learn something new and stumble onto something good. There are more possibilities than you think! Let's return to a point made earlier.

Better progress is made if you work out 10 variations of one piece or passage than one or two variations of ten pieces/passages. Ten variations force you to think, stretch, and develop stuff.

So let's do that right now! Below, I've modeled what to you could do by creating over a dozen ways to play a short passage. Each one isn't terrific. Each represents work, effort.

Example 10.14 Selected Passage for Development   *(Joyful, Joyful We Adore Thee)*

First, some "doubles" variations based on the previous chapter.

Example 10.15 Three "Doubles" Variations

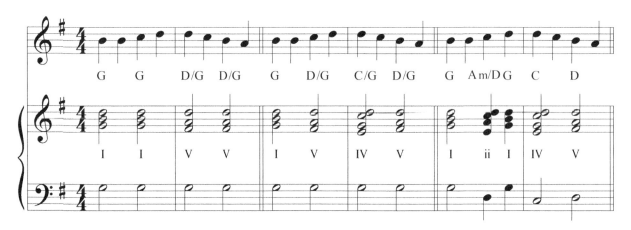

Example 10.16 Many More Ways are Possible

Suppose, and this ought to be our ultimate goal, we wanted to be more intentional and
"text paint" the following line of text?

Example 10.17

hearts   un - fold   like   flowers   be - fore   thee

Would the following possibilities begin to approach the imagery in the text?

Example 10.18

A.

B.

Are you convinced there are many possibilities? Let's review step 1.

Step 1. Impose limitations. Limit the soprano to scale degrees 1 and 5. We did that and created 22 possibilities. Not all of them were terrific.

Step 2. Remove the limitations. Let's demonstrate that.
Below, play the variation that we developed above. Note the inner Ab.

Example 10.19 Observe the Ab in the Inner Voice (Measure 1)

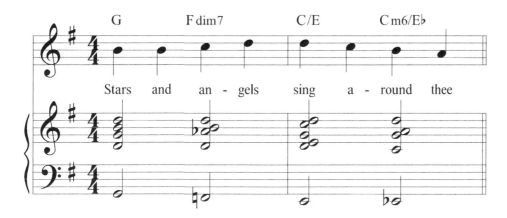

Example 10.20 The Ab placed an octave higher in the Soprano Voice (Measure 1)

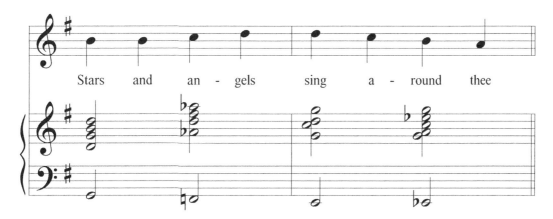

Play it. Isn't the result more dynamic, expressive? It leads us to consider more steps.

Step 3. Look for inner notes that could form an interesting line.

Step 4. Once you have generated a host of possibilities, pick out the best ones.

Step 5. Determine which ones go best together. Do they relate well together?

Now you have the beginnings of an arrangement! You have done some of the necessary preliminary work (research). You have some materials to work with.

Summing-Up

The examples demonstrated in this chapter are extreme! Consider again these practical ideas relative to letting go of the melody:
(1) Experiment. Center on scale degree 1 or 5 for one, two, or three measures rather than a whole stanza. Focus on the musical area that concerns you most.
(2) Relocate the top soprano note. Create a new line. Alter/revise the spacings.
(3) Focus on inner lines. Become more sensitive to the inner movement in chords.
(4) Change octaves. If you are working with scale degree 1, play it an octave higher or lower. A subtle change in tone color will result.

(5) Get out of a rut! Instead, *exhaust* the possibilities. *Force* yourself to explore and think in many, many new ways. Don't be so judgmental of your results. Some of the results won't be outstanding. That's OK.

(6) Position yourself for opportunities! When your attention is slavishly oriented to playing every note in the melody, you are constrained. You will likely miss opportunities to think orchestrally and to motivate congregational singing.

(7) *Text paint!* Seek to interpret the text musically. Vary the music to serve the text.

The above summary targets mainly harmony. Similar procedures could be applied to the shaping of rhythmic elements or finding melodic figures and lines, as below.

Riff Versions

A Different Approach. Riffs occur in contemporary worship music A riff is a short, repeated, rhythmic phrase, pattern, or melodic fragment.

Example 10.21 *How Great is Our God*

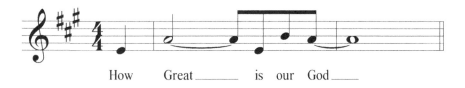

Below, a rhythmic riff centered on scale degree one, is repeated for eight measures as an accompaniment to the piece.

Example 10.22 Rhythmic Riff for *How Great is Our God*

Below, the riffs consist of two melodic variants, centered on the notes A and then B.

Example 10.23 Two Melodic Riffs

For the music below, first play only the riffs throughout. They occur in each of the 7 measures and provide the main melodic content. When you perform each, be sure to bring out the melodic riffs. Give each riff more weight than the other notes.

Fingering. The note E, scale degree 5, is sustained throughout by the RH baby finger. The RH thumb provides rhythmic movement and helps the lower "E" to ring. The LH provides the harmonic foundation.

Example 10.24 The Riffs Employed *(How Great is Our God)*

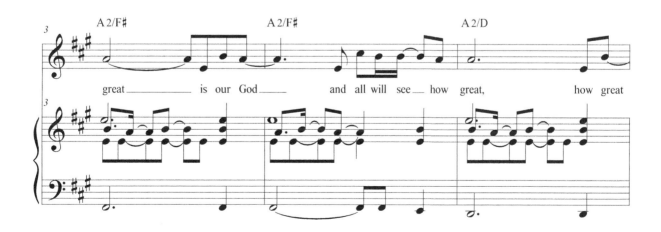

Observe, the major rhythmic/melodic activity occurs during the *long notes* of *How Great is Our God.* The long notes gave us space to create some counterpoint and still avoid clutter (too many things going on at the same time).

An A2 chord is maintained throughout. The bass falls stepwise to F# and D because any bass note in the major scale can sound good with an added second chord.

Example 10.25   A2 in Combination with the Bass Notes in the Scale

The riff utilizes, even highlights, the various sonic materials inherent in the A2 chord itself at different points.

Example 10.26 Sonic Elements Voicing the Riff Derived from A2

The result? From one seemingly static harmony (A2), melodic movement and rhythmic vitality is unloosed.

If you are playing in a band, your harmonic spacings will likely need to be leaner, with fewer doublings. If you are playing on a synth, always listen to what spacings sound good on each given preset. The result may sound be different than an acoustic piano.

Last Words. Coming back to the major purpose of this chapter, the basic question is this: "Do the people really *need* to hear the melody *all the time*?" Guitarists seldom play the melody at all, yet some are very effective worship leaders. Experiment! Acquire more freedom. Let go of the melody.

Test Time!

Have your teacher devise a test. Or do it yourself.

Possibilities
1. Play *Father I Adore You* (don't forget the sevenths) and *God is So Good* in the keys of C, D, E, F, G, and A.
2. Play *Amazing Grace* using Version A, or Version B (which employs the augmented fifth and sus9 chords), or Version C (Roman Numerals) in the keys of C, D, E, F, G, and A.
3. Play the chords for *Amazing Grace* in the keys of F and A. Retain scale degree 1 in the soprano part.
4. Continue the pattern. Play the sevenths through the descending fifth cycle.

Example 10.27 Major Seventh Pattern

Play the pattern starting with the C major seventh (as above) or a Db major seventh. The bass notes descend through the whole tone scale (eg., C, Bb, Ab, Gb, E, D, C).

"Glory and Honor"

If you are an aspiring worship keyboardist, you can't do better than to study and reflect on the book of Revelation. Fourteen of the twenty-two chapters deal with the primary struggle, worship. Who is to be worshiped, God or Satan?

A pair of wonderful words often go together: *glory and honor* (see 4:9, 11, 5:12, 13, 7:12, 21:26), which project the highest esteem and respect due God and the Lamb.

Since this pairing of words is so frequent in heaven, wouldn't it make sense to have them on our own lips (and take them to heart personally) as we play? Wouldn't it be wonderful if our hands could find a way to project the musical image of "glory."

Revoicing the Hymnbook

- 16 pages
- 24 examples

OUTLINE	REPERTOIRE
Revoicing what is on the Page	O God Our Help in Ages Past
Mix Chords & Single Melody Notes	Be Exalted, O God
Creating Contrast Using 2+2, 3+1, 3+2, 3+3, 4+2	Great is Thy Faithfulness
	To God Be The Glory
	Amazing Grace
	A Mighty Fortress
	Joyful, Joyful

This and the next chapter are addressed to keyboardists who can read hymnbook notation reasonably well. Drawing from the printed page itself, it conveys ways to begin to improvise. It is also dedicated to those who accompany congregational singing alone without a band. However, if you play in a band, you may be called on to play one stanza or repetition alone for contrast. This chapter will give you ideas on what to do.

How big is your hand? Can you stretch to an octave, a ninth, or a tenth? Easily? With difficulty? Or not at all? If your hand is small, you may have to make adjustments (as I often have to do). In fact, you may have to adjust some of the spacings in this and the next chapter. Sometimes a different fingering will solve the problem.

Not all four-note chords are equal for the hand! Some require a greater stretch. For example, B minor requires a greater stretch (is more tricky for small hands to perform) than C major. To prevent errors, a Bm triad or B5 open fifth may be safer, performance-wise.

Example 11.1a

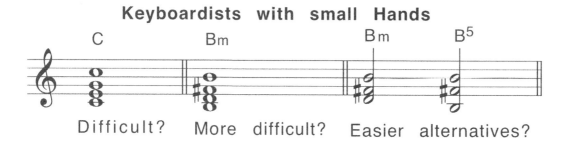

In this and the next chapter, therefore, instead of a four-note chord in the RH, you may want to play three notes and have your LH play middle "C" (as below).

Example 11.1b

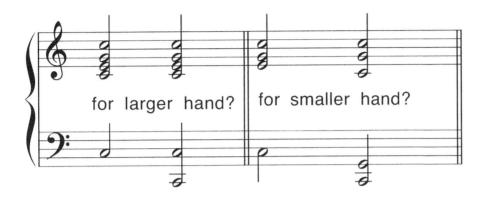

Again, this chapter is dedicated to those (1) who have great difficulty improvising, but can sight-read the hymnbook, note-for-note with relative ease, (2) who may be reading/playing from a hymnbook. A technique we'll use is 3+1, 3+2, and 4+2.

The three techniques require three-note chords in the right hand and one note or an octave in the left hand, or four-note chords in the RH and octaves in the LH.

Example 11.1c

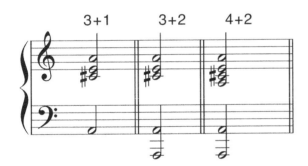

The 4+2 version results in the biggest, most powerful sound

Why are these spacing (voicing) alternatives important? Hymnbook settings are written for four-part singing—with two notes in the treble clef and two in the bass (2+2). Notes remain in the singing range, exclusively in the *middle* of the keyboard. They're *not* idiomatic to the piano. For greater effectiveness, keyboardists can *reorganize/revoice* what is on the page. By using different voicings, a more powerful, contrasting sound could result—without even changing the basic chord structure. This is a first step.

Also, this method helps you to become adept at quick, real-time chord analysis while you're in the act of reading and performing. Experienced improvisers (playing alone or in a band) do this kind of thing all the time. They are constantly reading ahead and figuring out the chord progressions that make up phrases. Once they have a good idea of what is on the page, they fashion their own voicings (or harmonies) on the spot. Let's look at the difference.

Example 11.2 Hymnbook Version *(Turn Your Eyes Upon Jesus)* **Play it!**

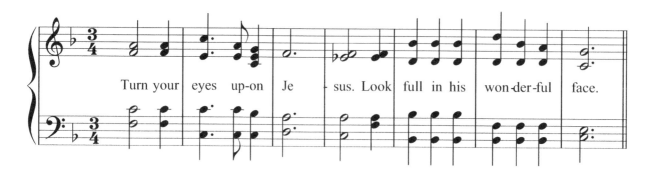

Example 11.3 3+1 Version   *(Turn Your Eyes Upon Jesus)* **Play it!**

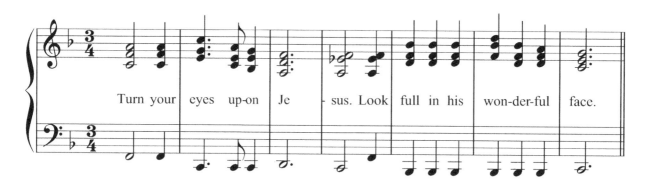

Revoicing What is On the Page

Analyze each chord below. Particularly note the *tenor part* and raise it an octave (when needed) so that a three-part chord results in your right hand. Drop the bass an octave.

Example 11.4 Hymnbook Version *(O God Our Help in Ages Past)*

Try it! Play it with three-note chords in the right hand and a single bass note in the left.
Tip. Often you'll need to raise the tenor part an octave and play it with your right hand.

Example 11.5 3+1 Version *(O God Our Help in Ages Past)*

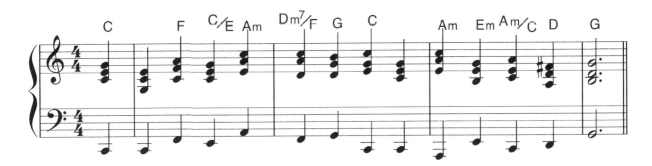

Example 11.6 4+2 Version (*O God Our Help in Ages Past*)

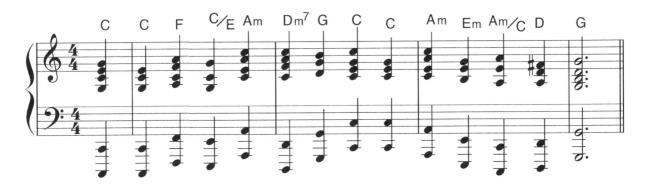

The majority of the chords in the RH are four note chords. A few are three note chords, for ease of performance. If we used only four note chords for the first three chords, our RH thumb would be required to jump from chord to chord and could cause an error or smudged note (especially if you have fat fingers). Therefore, *balance* the goal of using four note chords with the capacity of your RH.

Option For Small Hands (3+2)

Again, if you have small hands you may need to use even fewer octaves in the LH and fewer (or no) four-note chords in the RH. Three note chords in the RH and Octaves in the Bass (3+2) may be a better option. However if you can manage it, RH octaves with fifths (m.3, beat 3) are useful in projecting power. Moreover, try using some broken four-note chords as below (ms. 1+2).

Weak Fingers. Furthermore, if you have a large enough hand but weak fingers, you may need to strengthen them in order to play four-note chords with confidence.

Example 11.7 Basic 3+2 with No Four-Note Solid Chords in the Right Hand

Now perform the remainder of the piece below in the *3+1, 3+2, and 4+2* styles.

Example 11.8 Try it*! (O God our Help in Ages Past)*

Example 11.9 Try it! (*Doxology*)

Play it in the 3+1, 3+2, and 4+2 styles. Feel free to omit the eighth-note embellishments.

Example 11.10 Play it in the 3+1, 3+2 and 4+2 Styles *(A Mighty Fortress is Our God)*

Example 11.11 Play it in the 3+1, 3+2, and 4+2 Styles *(Great is Thy Faithfulness)*

Consider using 4+2 for at least part of the chorus.

Mix Chords & Single Melody Notes

Remember this thought. In general, we want to get the *maximum effect* with *the least amount of effort.* Often we need to simplify because we are busy making quick decisions in real time.

When full chords are played on each beat, songs can become clunky and ponderous. Sometimes eighth or sixteenth-note melody notes can be played as single notes or octaves without chords—or even omitted (m. 1). This makes performance much easier and we may not lose much musically. Also, avoid full chords on some of the weak beats. Use octave doublings in the right hand to give strong beats more emphasis. Try these ideas!

Example 11.12 Hymnbook Version *(To God Be The Glory)*

Your result should fall easily for your hand—be easy to play. Simplified, it could have looked and sounded like this.

Example 11.13 Simplified, Reorganized 3+1 Version *(To God Be The Glory)*

Try it! Now play the above using 4+2, but retaining the simplified format.

Example 11.14 *To God Be the Glory*   (4+2)

Try it! Close the book and play it using the hymnbook version, 3+1, and 4+2.

Below, the melody is maintained for the first two measures to reinforce the congregational singing, then dropped (G is retained in the soprano, ms. 3-5, 10-13). *Idea.* It's not necessary to play the melody all the way through a song.

Example 11.15 *Amazing Grace* (simplified with melody notes omitted)

Yes, this is simple! But it is a good starting place, and of course we could do more—and we will! Yet it is easy to play and works congregationally. Again, notice that the melody is retained for the first three measures, and then some melody notes are dropped. Why? Because once the melody is established the people may no longer need it to be reinforced.

Below, there will be times when you want a more powerful sound than what is below (so play it using 3+1, 4+2). However, the example is harder to utilize the 3+1, 4+2 strategy. So, play some of the tenor parts in the RH. This works well in measure one & two.

Example 11.16 Hymnbook Version (*Joyful, Joyful, We Adore Thee*)

Example 11.17 Simplified Chording. Big Sound (*Joyful, Joyful*)

Notice that we let go of parts of the melody, though the basic melodic line is still intact. Also we are stressing beats one and four, or two and four, rhythmically. The result is easy to play and is more majestic and powerful.

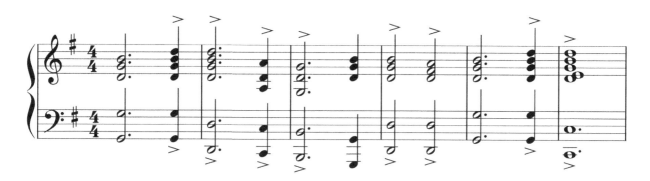

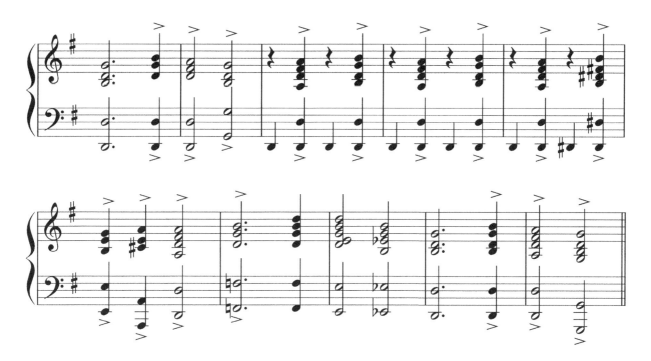

Try it! Play it again. This time add a few more melody notes with RH octaves. Below, we stress beats two and four even more by contrasting four note chords with open octaves. The "off-beats" on two and four create rhythmic energy.

Example 11.18 Rhythmic Alternative (*Joyful, Joyful*)

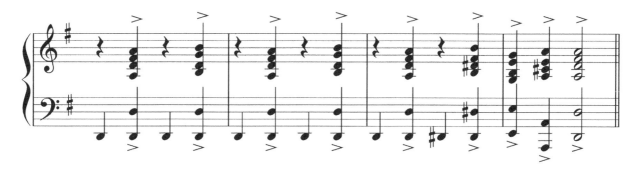

Try it! For variation, change the rhythmic pattern so that the accents fall on beats 1 and 3.

Example 11.19 Play it "As Is" *(Be Exalted, O God)*

I've noticed that students often stumble on the eighth notes. Solution? Simplify with octaves, and apply 4+2 overall. Your result could be like what follows.

Example 11.20 Reorganized 4+2 Version *(Be Exalted, O God)*

Were the octaves in the right and left hands easier to perform? Did they project strength?

Look at m2 (E/B, A/C#) and 3 (E/G#, B7/F#)). If the third or fifth of the chord is in the bass, a cleaner sound can be obtained by omitting the bass note from the right hand. That's the voicing principle used above, and illustrated immediately below.

Example 11.21 Right Hand Omits the Bass Note (G#)

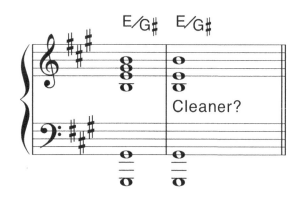

Measure two is not only cleaner. It is often easier to perform.

Creating Contrast 2+2, 3+1, 3+2, 3+3, 4+2

Some worship songs inherently possess dynamic contrast. They contain specific phrases that seem to call out for bigger, more dynamic sounds. This seems to be the case beginning in measures 9 and 17 below.

So start by playing the piece in it's hymnbook form, then switch to the *3+1 or 4+2 styles* for measures 9 and 17. Switch back and forth between the alternatives (including the hymnbook version) as needed to obtain sufficient dynamic contrast. Also think of fills you might use where you have long chords and plenty of space.

Analyze the text. What feelings are being expressed? Can you find ways to get at that?

Example 11.22 Hymnbook Version *(Be Still, My Soul)*

The hymnbook harmonies are gorgeous! For harmonic contrast, try using a pedal in the bass in the first lines (above). The following three variations may help you obtain some musical contrast. See if you like the effect.

Example 11.23 Use of Pedal in the Bass
A.

B. First Inversion Added Seconds at the End of the Phrase

C. Use of a Major Seventh & Higher Register Utilizing Chord Doublings

Example 11.24 Provide Big Down Beat for Climax *(Be Still My Soul)*

A. 4+2 Voicing

Above, a big-sounding, low octave on E, helps to set up the climax on the words, "Be still my soul." For emphasis, the bass octave could also be played an octave lower.

If you have a small hand, try these options (below). Consider doubling (thickening) the three-note E major triads for emphasis, or break up the four-note C# minor chord.

B. Options for Small Hands

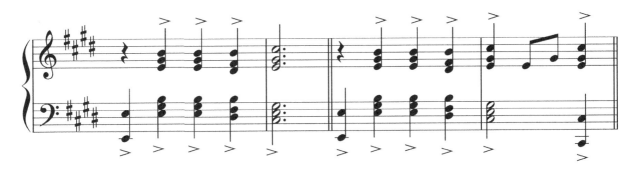

Main ideas
In this chapter we have demonstrated several ways of playing worship songs:
(1) using the hymnbook itself as a "blending" version (the middle of the keyboard)
(2) using the *3+1 style* for a more idiomatic keyboard approach
(3) using the 3+2 and *4+2 styles* to cut through textures for a more dynamic impact
(4) mixing chords with single melody notes for ease of performance
(5) simplifying/subtracting by omitting some melody notes and chords.

Reflect on this insightful definition of worship by the past Archbishop of Canterbury.

Worship is:
the quickening of the conscience by His holiness;
the nourishment of mind with His truth;
the purifying of imagination by His beauty;
the opening of the heart to His love;
the surrender of will to His purpose—
and all of this gathered up in adoration, the most selfless emotion
of which our nature is capable and therefore the chief remedy for that
self-centeredness which is our original sin and the source of all actual sin.
William Temple
Archbishop of Canterbury

Revitalizing the Hymnbook

- 14 pages
- 25 examples

OUTLINE	REPERTOIRE
Cut Through with Octaves and Tenths	To God Be The Glory
Provide Dynamic Harmonic Alternatives	And Can it Be
Supply Motivating Fills	Rejoice the Lord is King
Create Some Movement!	

The chapter imparts specific techniques designed to motivate congregational singing.
It is dedicated to those (1) who have great difficulty improvising, but can sight-read the
hymnbook, note-for-note with relative ease, (2) who may be reading directly from a
hymnbook and playing alone, (3) who may be playing in a band and are asked, for the
sake of contrast, to perform a verse or chorus repetition alone, and (4) who desire help
and practice in creating "fills."

Cut Through with Octaves and Tenths

Let's take a closer look at what we need to do to *motivate* the people to sing with gusto.
To make this happen, we have to become somewhat of a musical psychologist.

Example 12.1 Hymnbook Version *(To God Be The Glory)*

Try it! Let's focus on the chorus of To God be the Glory. For the first two measures of the climactic chorus ("Praise the Lord"), create *five different ways* of playing it.

We will want the keyboard to really cut through, grab everyone's attention, and motivate everyone to sing those high notes (B-C-D). Look at some solutions.

See the use of *octaves* and *doubled octaves*. On the second line, "Let the" is omitted. Very little is lost in this simplification, and the result is much easier to play. Subtraction!

Example 12.2 Reorganized Versions (*To God Be the Glory*)

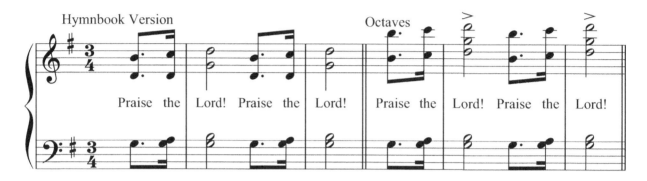

Again, on "Let the", the keyboard is silent. Not playing at all makes it easier to perform the G chord on the word "earth" with confidence. On "earth hear His voice" the melody is omitted. Instead, with the D's on top, a more insistent quality results. It's also easier to play and causes the congregation no problem—they can still sing the melody with ease.

Tenths are often a good idea. Below, tenths between the bass and treble clefs creates an even more powerful sound. Or, make it even more simple. Play just octaves in both hands.

Example 12.3 Octaves a Tenth Apart or Just Doubled Octaves

Above, feel free to use single notes in the LH and RH hands (two octaves apart) for the second half of the example. You won't lose much and it will be much easier technically.

Example 12.4 A Harmonic Variation

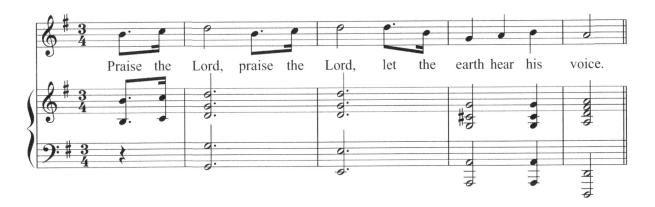

Praise the Lord, praise the Lord, let the earth hear his voice.

Provide Dynamic Harmonic Alternatives

Example 12.5 Hymnbook Version

Try it! Provide five harmonic alternatives for the above excerpt.

Example 12.6 A Harmonic Variation

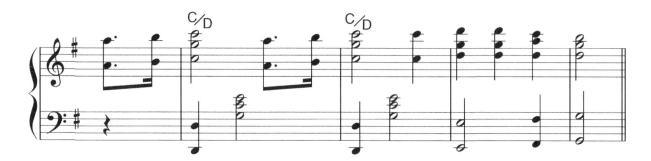

Example 12.7 Another Harmonic Variation

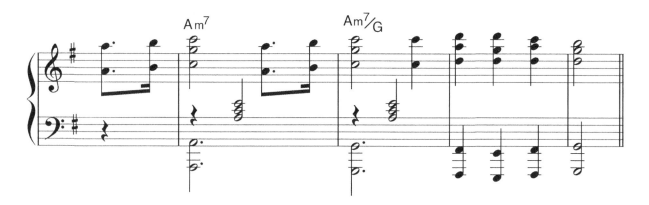

Example 12.8 Some Bass Movement in Chorus of *To God be the Glory*

Try octaves in the bass. Notice the RH is inactive while the LH is active—a good idea.

Supply Motivating Fills

Another issue. We need to create a "fill" — we need some energy and movement —just prior to the chorus. The fill should prepare the people to sing out with power.

Example 12.9 Provide Some Energy Before the Chorus *(To God be the Glory)*

Try it! Create five fills. First create 5 fills for the RH. Then five fills for the LH.

Example 12.10 Representative Fills for the Right Hand

The treble clef fills could be played with octaves.

Try it! Create 5 bass fills. When your LH is active, it's usually a good idea for your RH *not* to be active.

We have focused on the chorus of *To God be the Glory* where increased musical activity needs to take place in order to motivate the congregation to sing out. We turn to another topic.

Create Some Movement!

The refrain of *And Can It Be* cries out for a bolder treatment. Here is the hymnbook version. It's tailor-made for singers, but not idiomatic for keyboardists.

Example 12.11 Refrain of Hymnbook Version of *And Can it Be*

Try it! Try to create something with a bigger sound, and more keyboard energy. Consider creating some bass movement by walking up stepwise? This takes more skill, but let's look at some examples.

Example 12.12 Bigger Sound Using Octaves and Bass Movement *(And Can It Be)*

Above, the bass notes D, E, F#, and G, A, B walk up to the first inversion chord. Now, below, let's extend the movement in the bass a little more.

Example 12.13 Ascending Lines Employing Tenths (*And Can it Be*)

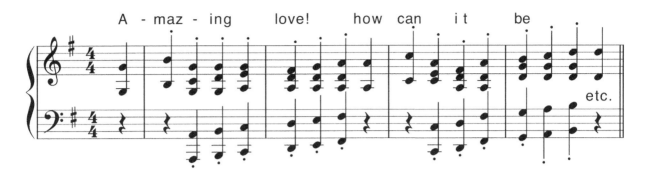

Did you see the tenths? Look for them! Tenths are really important! In measure one they are somewhat hidden between the alto and bass parts, yet play a vital role.

Example 12.14 Tenths Exposed *(And Can it Be)*

Play it! Close the book. Play by memory the piece with both kinds of tenths in F and G.

Now let's experiment with another idea. Let's attempt to create more rhythmic energy by using off-beats. If you know Beethoven's' music, you will immediately recognize that he uses this idea often.

Remember! Our whole point in creating these variations is to inspire the people to sing with more conviction and energy.

Example 12.15 Off-Beats on Two and Four Create Energy *(And Can It Be)*

Question? Why were three accented chords rising stepwise employed in measure four?

By creating some energy and movement, we sought to motivate the congregation to "go for it" and to sing the high "E" of measure five, the highest note in the piece.

Example 12.16 Complete the Chorus using Rhythmic Off -Beats on Two and Four.

Try it! Can you sustain the idea? Try the refrain employing similar rhythmic ideas.

Another way to create energy is to create an energizing bass line. This is easier said than done, but later in the book we'll work on ways to create bass lines. Below the bass part creates forward tension by descending chromatically using half-steps from F to B.

Example 12.17 Chromatic Bass Line (*And Can it Be*)

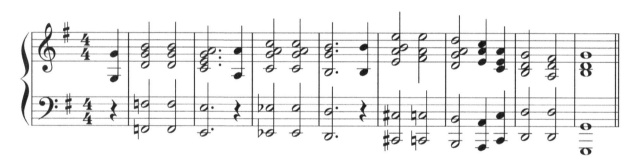

However, the above example may feel too static rhythmically. *Do something about it!*

Try it! Create more bass movement. Create so accents fall on beats two and four.

Example 12.18 Movement (off-beats) in the Bass (*And Can it Be*)

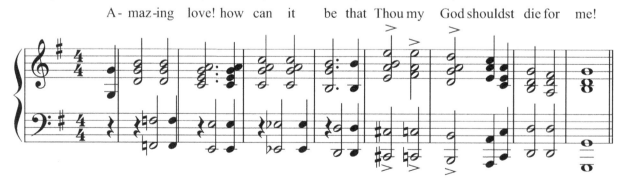

Do you feel that the above harmonization enhances the meaning of the words?

Try it! Vary it. Now play the above passage but put accents on beats one and three.

Example 12.19 Provide the Foundational Chords *(And Can it Be)*

Above, if the congregation is *secure* in singing the broken chords in the melody (perhaps by the third stanza), the forceful block chords can bring energy to the phrase.

On the other hand, if the congregation is *insecure* during stanza one or two, bring out the melody with octaves. Since the octaves in the RH pose some difficulty technically, avoid jumps in the LH. Keep the LH simple.

Example 12.20 Octaves in the Melody *(And Can it Be)*

If the people need even more help with the melody, or the RH octaves are too difficult, create octaves using single, melody notes in each hand. Forget the chords.

In Rejoice the Lord is King (below), a quarter note feel occurs in the bass, and chordal spikes in the RH. The bass part is active, whereas the RH is relatively inactive. This sort of contrast is often a good idea. It makes improvisation easier: there's less to think about For a more dynamic emphasis, the RH could employ more octaves (a fuller sound).

Example 12.21 Movement in the Bass & Spikes in RH (*Rejoice the Lord is King*)

Below, the slightly different alternative is less chromatic, and more diatonic.

Example 12.22 *Rejoice the Lord is King* (Active, but More Diatonic Alternative)

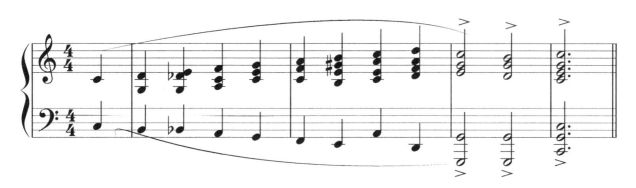

Below, the "subtraction principle" is in play. Fewer notes and fewer harmonic changes result in a less flowing, but more dynamic alternative. The keyboard spacings are wider and bolder. And overall, the passage is easier to perform.

Example 12.23 Subtraction Principle with Wider Spacing (Less Active, More Effective?)

While three or four chord changes per measure present no problem to the keyboardist, guitarists desire fewer chord changes, one or two per measure, in order to maintain a sense of flow. Below, see a harmonically simplified, guitar version.

Example 12.24 Guitar Friendly Version (Harmonic Activity Greatly Reduced)

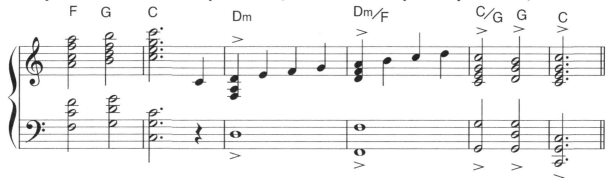

Observe another bare-bones, idiomatic, keyboard treatment (below) intended to help spur congregational singing. Notice the melody is alluded to but not followed slavishly.

Example 12.25 *Rejoice the Lord is King*

Main ideas. In the two "Hymnbook" chapters we have demonstrated several ways of playing worship songs:

(1) using the hymnbook as is. It blends in nicely. In contrast, the *3+1 style (more idiomatic to the keyboard), and the 3+2 and 4+2 styles* (which cut through textures more forcibly) have a more dynamic impact.

(2) mixing chords with single melody notes

(3) simplifying or subtracting by omitting some melody notes and chords

(4) creating fills for the purpose of motivating praise

(5) using octaves and tenths to cut through textures

(6) and fashioning dynamic, alternative harmonies

Commit yourself to learning one new thing each week.
Concentrate on a single measure, phrase, or harmonic progression.
Explore the possible voicings of a single chord.
Don't feel you must practice a whole piece.

Become a life-long learner.

PLAYING KEYBOARDS IN A WORSHIP BAND

The Worhip Band—A Different Animal!

Stylistically, the chapters that follow take a sharp turn in a different direction. The previous two chapters addressed "what is possible" when playing the piano *by yourself* at home, or when playing or leading worship from the keyboard alone *by yourself,* for instance, you have more freedom, especially harmonically.

However, playing in a worship band requires rethinking your role—*how* and *what* you should play. It involves finding a part that works with the other players and serves the whole.

Can Less Be More?

Think of a symphony orchestra or a film track. At various points in a film track we may hear only the strings, the percussion, the brass, or the winds. Even a single instrument all alone. Not everyone plays all the time. Embrace that principle in worship! For example, in a rehearsal, you could be asked to cut in half what you're playing—to see if the net result is more effective. That could be personally embarrassing! Nevertheless, try to respond without getting "hurt" or feeling personally demeaned. The "whole effect" is the paramount thing. Demonstrate a willingness to play less, and if it's beneficial to the whole, even play just a few notes!

The 100% Rule. If we have four instruments in our band, it should be obvious that all four players cannot have the dominant, lead part at the same time. There has to be a give and take. If one person is allotted 60% of the "pie," the other three have to share the remaining 40%. There is only so much musical space available. Player roles can change from piece to piece. In a guitar-driven piece, the keyboardist may provide only minimal background support. In an intimate piece, the drummer may just play brushes. In the "break down" the drummer may play alone. Or, the entire band may sit out as the congregation sings a cappella.

Contrast is vital! Dynamic contrast is vital in our worship and contrast is demonstrated in the worship in heaven, designed by God Himself. Three concentric circles of praise around the throne are evident. A crescendo of praise builds, erupts, resounds. First in Revelation chapter 4 and 5, the four living creatures respond (4:8), then the 24 elders (4:10), then the four creatures and 24 elders together (5:8), then the angels (5:11), and finally every living creature (5:13)—*all* of heaven, every creature in heaven, on earth, and under the earth is shouting as praise rises. Heaven's worship is full of contrast! Revelation's worship reveals thought, planning, and structure. We could learn from that. We should add too, worship in heaven is emotional. Note the seven-fold, repetitive exaltation (5:12). We hear loud voices, sounds like "many waters." Add some thunder. Yes, it's in there. Read it!

The groove. When playing or leading alone, "rubato" (an elastic, slight speeding up or slowing down of the tempo) is easy to employ and can be very effective. But in a band, it's more difficult. In contemporary worship the groove becomes more important.

The "groove" is the combined, in-sync effort of the rhythm section players when beat and rhythm come together coherently. Often it means not speeding up when you become excited or slowing down in soft, tranquil passages. So, when practicing at home, consider using a metronome. Study your own rhythmic tendencies (we all have them)–otherwise you may not know them. Likely, some day you will be required to play in sync with a track at church, given current technology.

Consider these essential guidelines for playing the keyboard in a worship band.

Keyboard Guidelines

Listen to the drums, bass, and guitar parts!

1. If the kick is busy, then the left hand of the keyboardist needs to be simple. Listen to the Hi-Hat. It tells you the "feel." Do you hear 8ths or 16ths?
2. If the bass is busy, then the keyboard LH needs to be simple. And vice versa. Trade off!
3. If the guitar is busy, then the keyboard needs to be simple. And vice versa. Trade off! If the guitar strums throughout, play more.

You will find these principles being observed in the recorded examples played by the band in the following chapters.

If the worship piece is new or unfamiliar to the people, yes, by all means bring out the melody.
If you have two keyboards on stage, one should be less busy.

A Major Challenge. One of the most formidable challenges facing keyboardists is to have sufficient mastery of their instrument, and in addition, the extra capacity to not only listen to themselves, but also (at the same time) *listen to the band.* A seasoned, LA session player shared with me, "With my left ear I listen to myself. With my right ear I listen to the band."

REALLY TUNE INTO THESE THOUGHTS. TAKE THEM SERIOUSLY.

About the Recorded Band Pieces. In the chapters that follow, the keyboard and band performances were improvised in real time from the charts that are provided. A notated piano part is provided, so you can learn it and play along. The harmonies are traditional, very similar to what you might find in a hymnbook. Most of the songs, *God is So Good, Amazing Grace, Great is Thy Faithfulness, Joyful, Joyful We Adore Thee,* have been dealt at least in part in previous chapters. You'll get a different perspective of them.

The keyboard parts are designed for the intermediate pianist. If a keyboard part is too challenging in a particular place—if you encounter a fast, ornamental turn, for example— simplify or omit it and continue. Throughout, broken chords, runs, scalar passages, and fills are intentionally fashioned to fall easily for your hand. Piano pedals are not indicated. Listen to the tracks for the appropriate amount of pedal.

We'll Understand It Better Bye and Bye

Unique chapter organization. This chapter and those following are organized differently than previous ones. A complete song (not a fragment) is presented. Be sure to learn the notated keyboard part (below) and play it with the band track.

Keyboard Pads. In much of the guitar and drum-driven worship occurring today, the keyboard tends to function in a backing, even fringe role. Some of our keyboardists provide background, "underscoring" music during prayer, ministry time, talking transitions, and altar calls. In congregational pieces, keyboardists with technical ability are playing simple atmospheric pads, sometimes with one hand. Similarly, some of our guitar students double at the "keys," having become adept at playing simple pads that sit underneath the basic texture, filling in the space, helping it feel warm, full.

Example 14.1 *Well Understand It Better Bye and Bye*

Our first piece, a happy, old-time, Gospel song, has some of these qualities. The backing Rhodes part provides atmosphere and the basic chordal foundation, whereas the guitar generally has a busier, active role. The piece observes an important principle: when the guitar is active, the keyboard needs to be simple. Notice, a solid groove is established. The guitar and bass parts are notated for the first 10 measures so you can see the parts.

Doxology

This short piece, the *Doxology*, employs traditional, classical-like harmonies similar to what you'd find in a hymnbook. Learn the notated piano part and then play along with the band tracks (available online). The following options are available:

Choose from two scores: (1) piano only score (2) band chart.
Choose from four tracks: (a) vocal, band, piano; (b) band
with piano; (c) piano only; (d) band without piano.

Suggestion. Once you have learned the piano part, play along with the band track that omits the keyboard (track d).

Consider the following keyboard guidelines for playing effectively in a band. We'll continue to discuss this issue in the following band chapters.

Keyboard Guidelines

Use less doubling. Employ thinner, leaner textures. In a previous chapter, *Revitalizing the Hymnbook,* we assumed we were playing or leading alone. One of our goals was to have big, powerful sounds, and to take full advantage of the entire range of the keyboard in order to direct, mold, and inspire the congregational singing. Therefore, we included three and four-note chords in the RH, octaves in the LH, and chord doublings, like those below.

Example 15.1 Powerful Spacings When Playing Alone (3+2, 4+2)

But when playing in a band, non-doubled, lean voicings are often more appropriate. In general, use two or three-note chords in the RH. Shell voicings, which omit the fifth, are often ideal (see chapter 6). Look at the leaner voicings below.

Example 15.2 Leaner Voicings for Playing in a Band

Four notes in the RH with octaves, or three notes in each hand, might be admissible if the song is loud and "concerto-ish." But even then, not through the entire song, especially if the guitar is playing chords. Too many notes and doublings result in clutter.

During the *Doxology* introduction (below), the piano takes the leads and plays solid three-note chords in the RH, for it has the primary, declaiming role. After that, a more linear treatment occurs (ms. 6-8) with the piano bass part staying out of the range of the bass (for the most part). Solid chords return at the very end of the piece.

Example 15.3 *Doxology* Keyboard Part [Problem of Vocal or NO vocal names]

Notice the ritard at the end.

The recorded keyboard and band performances were improvised using the band chart below. Experiment! Create your own part and play along with the band using track D.

Example 15.4 *Doxology* (Band Chart)

God Is So Good

This short piece, *God is So Good*, employs traditional, classical-like harmonies similar to what you'd find in a hymnbook. Learn the notated piano part and then play along with the band tracks (available online). The following options are available:

Choose from two scores: (1) piano only score (2) band chart.

Choose from four tracks: (a) vocal, band, piano; (b) band with piano; (c) piano only; (d) band without piano.

Suggestion. Once you have learned the piano part, play along with the band track that omits the keyboard (track d).

Keyboard Notes

In the previous piece, the Doxology, the lightly embroidered keyboard part kept close to the melody. In contrast, *God is so Good (below)* bypasses much of the melody. In measures 3 through 9 and 13 through 17, unique lines are fashioned (session players call them "fills"). You'll recall that we spent time with *God is So Good* in chapter four. Revisit chapter four and compare that treatment with this one.

Example 16.1 *God is So Good*   (Keyboard Part)

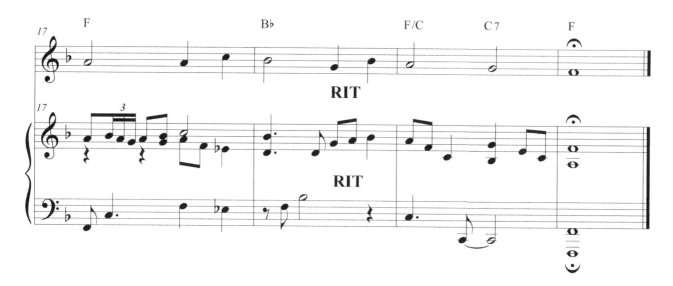

Notice the ritard at the end.

The recorded keyboard and band performances were improvised using the lead sheet chart below. Experiment! Create your own part and play along with the band using track D.

Example 16.2 *God is So Good* (Band Chart)

Silent Night

Two scores are provided: (1) piano only notation (2) band chart.

Silent Night has four tracks: (a) vocal, band, piano; (b) band with piano; (c) piano only; (d) band without piano.

Suggestions. Learn the piano part (track c). Play the piano part with the band without the piano track (track d).

Keyboard Spacings When Playing in a Band

Use less doubling. Employ thinner, leaner textures. When playing or leading worship by alone by ourselves in a previous chapter, *Revitalizing the Hymnbook,* we took full advantage of the entire range of the keyboard, and employed big, powerful sounds in order to direct, mold, and inspire the congregational singing. Using the spacings below, we utilized three and four-note chords in the RH, octaves in the LH, and used chord doublings.

Example 17.1 Powerful Spacings for Playing Alone (3+2, 4+2, 3+3)

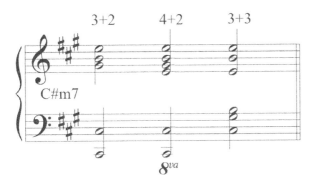

But when playing in a band, leaner voicings are often more appropriate. In the piano part of *Silent Night*, see the various C#m7 spacings that are employed.

Example 17.2 Less Doubling and Leaner Voicings When Playing in a Band

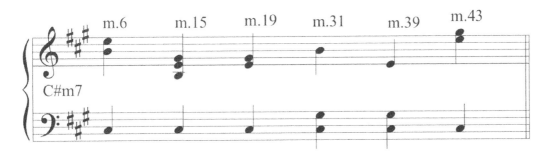

Too many notes and too many doublings tend to result in clutter.
In general, piano parts can be busier than Rhodes parts.

Example 17.3 *Silent Night* (Keyboard Part)

Piano Notes. Very little chord doubling occurs in the piano part. Chord progressions with descending fifths occur in both verses (ms. 7-11, 19-22, 31-35, 43-46), avoiding in ms. 7-11 what might have been four measures of a static A major chord. Contrary motion, often a good idea, occurs twice in the melody lines (ms. 18-20, 41-44). Where there are "holes," that is, where the melody is inactive or notes are relatively long, fills are employed (ms. 23-24, 30, 32). Economy of means is demonstrated: no more notes are played than what is needed.

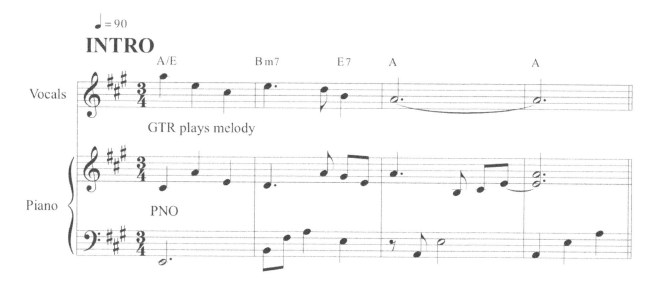

The recorded keyboard and band performances were improvised using the band chart below. Experiment! Create your own part and play along with the band using Track D.

Example 17.4 *Silent Night* (Band Chart)

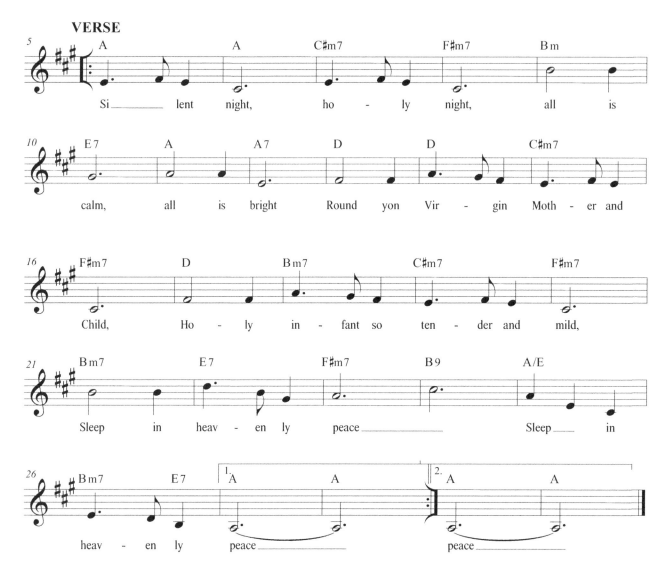

Did you play the piano part alongside the band? Did you create your own piano part?

Amazing Grace

Two scores are provided: (1) piano only notation (2) band chart.

Four tracks are provided: (a) vocal, band, piano; (b) band
with piano; (c) piano only; (d) band without piano.

Suggestions. Learn the piano part (track c). Play the piano part with the track that omits the
piano (track d).

Shuffle Rhythm Introduced. For the first stanza, even eights are employed. For the second
stanza, shuffle eights (uneven, swung eights) occur. Note also the gospel licks in measures 21
and 29-30 of the second stanza. For a more detailed perspective on gospel stylings, compare
these with the "Gospel Doubles" and "Gospel Extensions" in chapter nine, and the shuffle
version of *Amazing Grace* in chapter four. Measures 30-31 have a tidbit of Country.

Example 18.1 *Amazing Grace* Even Eights (Stanza 1) followed by Shuffle Eights (Stanza 2)

Example 18.2   *Amazing Grace* Create Your Part. Play Along With Track D.

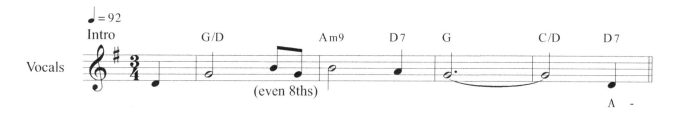

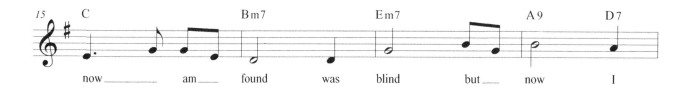

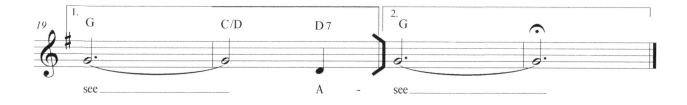

Great Is Thy Faithfulness

The classic hymn, *Great is Thy Faithfulness*, receives a lot of attention in the *Keyboard Worship* series. Altogether, the four books communicate an abundance of ways to approach the hymn harmonically. Here, however, traditional hymnbook harmonies are closely followed, and a Baroque, classical-like style is employed.

Two scores are provided: (1) piano notation (2) band chart.

Four tracks are provided: (a) vocal, band, piano; (b) band with piano; (c) piano only; (d) band without piano.

Suggestions. Be sure to learn the piano part (track c). Play the piano part along with the track that omits the piano (track d).

Things to notice. A basic principle is demonstrated in measures 13-16 and 29-32: when the RH hand is busy, the LH is simple. Chord inversions are used as fills (ms. 53-54). At measure 61, the 16th note embellishment is fashioned to fall easily for the hand. Throughout, the RH spacings consist of two or three notes—thick chord doublings are minimized.

Example 19.1 *Great is Thy Faithfulness* (Keyboard Part)

A - Verse 1

B - Chorus

C- INTERLUDE

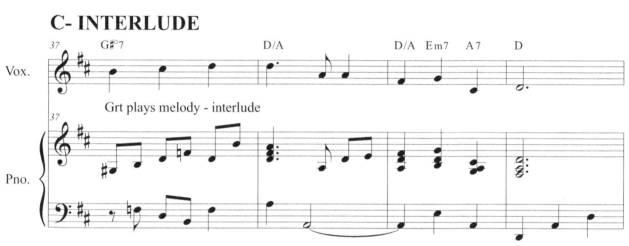

Grt plays melody - interlude

D -VERSE 2

Example 19.2 *Great is Thy Faithfulness* (Band Chart)

Create your part. Play along with track D.

VERSE

CHORUS

Joyful, Joyful We Adore Thee

In chapter 10 we explored many ways to harmonize the first phrase of *Joyful, Joyful We Adore Thee.* In chapter 11, we used the basic hymnbook harmonies and applied 3+1, 3+2, and 4+2 chord spacings, as well other ways to create a big sound and create rhythmic interest. Here, playing in a band, the same hymnbook harmonies occur within a Classical-Baroque style. The keyboard part is slightly more difficult than the previous band pieces.

Two scores are provided: (1) piano notation (2) band chart.

Four tracks are provided: (a) vocal, band, piano; (b) band
with piano; (c) piano only; (d) band without piano.

Suggestions. Learn the piano part (track c). Play the piano part with track d.

Example 20.1 *Joyful, Joyful, We Adore Thee* (Keyboard Score)

B - INTERLUDE

C - Verse 2

20.2 *Joyful, Joyful We Adore* Thee (Band Score)

Create your own keyboard part. Play along with track D.

The band charts in Book 2 are more challenging pianistically, more diverse, and more contemporary in style.

Other Books in Keyboard Series

(All Books Under $10)

Keyboard Worship Book 2 of 4
Contemporary Chord Colors

This book looks at the new, current, harmonic expansions which help give contemporary worship its modern sound, and how to integrate and apply them.

300 Online Tracks Included
Tracks for Playing Along with a Worship Band
Musical ideas embedded in well-known worship songs

Who is the Book for?
Intermediate to Advanced keyboardists desiring to sound contemporary
College worship major keyboardists
Classical pianists who want to improvise but don't know how

Basic Competencies Addressed
Infuse colors, resonances, character into worship expression
Integrate Drones, Added Seconds, Slash Chords into your artistic pallet
Uncover the usefulness of Quartals (4th chords), rootless sonorities
Substitute Sus, "Four over Five," and "One over Four" chords into worship songs
Give classic hymns & choruses a fresh look
Techniques for playing in a worship band

Keyboard Worship Book 3 of 4
Advanced Harmonic Techniques

This book addresses established harmonic techniques that are well known and appear in Broadway music, film scores, and Jazz, but are not well understood or used by most contemporary worship keyboardists.

In-Depth Panorama of Harmonic Possibilities
Advanced Level
300 Online Tracks Included

Who is the Book for?
College Undergraduate and Graduate Worship Keyboard Majors
College Undergraduate and Graduate Classical Piano Majors
Keyboardists with the hunger, drive, to train and perform for the glory of God

Goals

See your congregation sing with energy and conviction

Bring out the theology in worship songs

Create interesting bass/melody lines, captivating harmonies

Develop arranging and collaborating skills

Competencies Addressed

Learn to "text paint"—bring out theology in worship songs

Apply Secondary Dominants, Altered Dominants, Diminished, Half Diminished Sevenths

Employ tri-tone substitutions, half-step tensions, inner voice leading

Revoice extensions—evoke bold, nuanced colors

Devote all the powers of art to instill in classic hymns/worship songs vitality—spirit!

Create inspiring accompaniments for singers and instrumentalists

Keyboard Worship Book 4 of 4 (forthcoming)
Modulation, Intros, Outros, Turn Arounds

This book explores different ways to integrate and apply modulations, intros, outros and turnarounds.

200 Online Tracks Included

Advanced Level

Tracks for Playing Along with Worship Accompaniments

Musical ideas embedded in well-known worship songs

Who is the Book for?

Worship leaders and keyboardists seeking to fashion effective transitions

College Undergraduate and Graduate Keyboard Majors

Competencies Addressed

Ways of achieving free-flowing, seamless worship

Short and long modulations within and between songs

Modulations involving songs in different keys and with different meters

The value of Sus substitutions in creating modulations and intros

Emotionally meaningful modulations, intros, outros, turn arounds

All book sales donated to a children's orphanage in India
("Vikasitha Ministries")

Announcements and Resources
at *WorshipInfo.com*

Worshipinfo.com

Worshipinfo.com is the "headquarters" for announcements concerning the *Keyboard Worship* Series.

Downloadable mp3 Examples

Free, downloadable mp3 files for the *Keyboard Worship* books are available at worshipinfo. com. Approximately 90% of the music examples are public domain and presented without any limitations. For the remaining 10%, the copyrighted examples, licenses were obtained for the published books. However, to comply with copyright restrictions regarding the audio files, full mp3 accompaniments are provided, but the melodies have been omitted. Nevertheless, since both the melodies and melody accompaniments are notated in the books, this should not be a serious drawback.

Book Four

When *Book Four—Modulations, Intros, Outros, Turn Arounds*, becomes available, an announcement will be made at worshipinfo.com. Worshipinfo.com will be our announcement headquarters.

Other Forms Projected for the *Keyboard Worship* Series

As time and energy permits and technological challenges are overcome, announcements will be made of the following forms of the *Keyboard Worship* series, when and if they become available:

    A.   Midiculous Version

    B.   Ebook Version

    C.   Youtube Lessons

What is Midiculous.com?

Midiculous software allows those who do not read music notation to hear and view the music examples being played on an 88-note keyboard displayed on your computer screen. As you hear the music examples played, you will see the piano keys being depressed visually in real time. You can slow down or speed up the examples, change keys, view the chord symbols, and play along. This exciting software is free to users (visit the site). It should enable *Keyboard Worship* to reach out and bless a large group of keyboardists who play by ear but read music notation hesitantly or not at all. Our expectation is that the book version along with the midiculous version, together, will reinforce each other and help ease the learning process. For that reason, the development of a midiculous component is a high priority.

Browse Worshipinfo.com

An abundance of downloadable materials, worship articles, worship PowerPoints used in my university teaching, and other sundry tools, are available free of charge—approximately 185 files in all. Additionally, the web sites of our Biola worship faculty (guitar, piano, bass, drums, voice, technology) are posted.

Finally, I want to draw your attention to two other keyboard books by friends of mine: *Worship Piano* by Bob Kauflin (Hal Leonard, 2017), and *The Complete Church Pianist* by Debbie Denke (2011).

A Personal Note

Looking at outward circumstances only, it would seem very unlikely that I would be a music professor, no less a Ph.D., and be writing this or any book.

I grew up in Vancouver BC in a loving, musical family, located in a poor, lower-class district of the city. My dad had a grade four education and I think my mom made it to grade ten. My parents respected education, but had no concept of higher education. My dad, who could barely read, had a small auto body shop, straightened fenders and painted cars. After school my brother and I would bicycle to dad's shop and help him. We loved our dad!

So how did it happen that I became a Ph.D? I give major credit to my home church and our pastor, W.H. Brooks, whom I loved and admired. Religiously, and without fail, our family attended sunday school and every morning and evening service. Pastor Books brought in a lot of missionaries and guest preachers (some were really good) that opened up the world to me.

Nurtured and lifted up in this enlightening environment, I can remember, as a teenager, having one thought as I tried to contemplate my future. This one phrase stuck in my mind: "I want to make a contribution!" I had no idea what that might be.

My avid interest in music came mostly from my dad and an incident that happened at church. Though my mom loved music and could play the piano, dad was the chief inspirer of music in our home. He sang, played, built instruments, and started tape recording my brother Don and me singing, well before we reached school age.

I began taking piano lessons at the age of 7 or 8, but when I was 12 a guy my age, Franklyn Lacey, came to our Sunday evening service and improvised on the piano. He stunned and amazed me. I went home and started working on it. Within a year I could play like Franklyn. I developed some piano solos and got to play one during the Sunday evening offering.

Dad sensed I needed a teacher who could help me. I will never forget the first meeting I had with Rowlie Hill, the best-known Christian piano teacher in the city. Teaching at his home, Rowlie said, "Play something for me." I played him my most expressive solo, with runs up and down the keyboard. "Very good," he said. Then he put music on the piano, "Read this." Immediately I broke down and wept uncontrollably. I said, "I can't do it…I just can't do it." It was so embarrassing to be a thirteen-year-old and to sob so uncontrollably. But I couldn't help myself. Years later Rowlie told me, "Right then, I knew you were a musician because of the way it affected you." That's one of the reasons, incidentally, why I've always been sympathetic to improvisers who struggle to read.

Soon after, I *really needed* to read! Our church invited me to play the piano (along with the organist) at our evening song service which was always packed with about 600 people. The ability to play a piano solo may have appeared impressive to our people, but I don't think they had any idea how raw, ignorant, and unprepared I was.

It was scary! I never knew what songs they'd pick. My anxiety rose as the service time approached. I'd get up there and "hope" I could play the key in the hymnbook. I knew some better than others. I didn't want to make a fool out of myself. I could read a little, but not fluently or securely. I mostly listened to the harmonies played on the organ and doodled on the first stanza. By the second and third stanza I had a better idea. The sheer terror of Sunday nights motivated me to learn how to read music—and fast!

The Sunday nights I wasn't playing, Rowlie drove all the way across town to our home (that always impressed me), and picked me up so I could be the accompanist for his youth choir. While driving me home, Rowlie would impress upon me the importance of serving in the church.

Around that time, I met Tom Keene, his most gifted student, also a christian. Tom and I went to high school together for a year, talked music every lunch hour, and became life-long friends. Unaware of any keyboard books, secular or sacred, we began taking down recordings note-for-note—records by Ted Smith (who played for Billy Graham), and other guys— and played them back note-for-note.

"What were our lives like those days?" We played at different services and youth meetings, at Youth for Christ competitions, and accompanied trios and quartets. Tom got to play on a 30 minute "live" radio program every Sunday night on CJOR. It was a big deal! In the summers, I began playing for small-city, evangelistic tent campaigns, Barry Moore city-wide crusades across Canada, and eventually a Leighton Ford/Billy Graham two-week crusade in Vancouver which filled up our Empire Stadium with 30,000 people.

Tom went on to Junior College in Washington, transferred, graduated from Biola where I now teach, and became a LA studio musician. He's arranged and performed on more than a 1000 recordings, and wrote the band arrangements in this book, improvising the piano parts.

I went the academic route. How it happened was amazing and may be important to you. While I was a music student at the University of British Columbia, the department head, Dr. Marquis, called me into his office: "Barry, have you thought about graduate school?" I was shocked as I wasn't sure I was of that caliber. "Think about it. Talk to your parents. We'll need a little money for applications. If this seems right, come back and see me."

I came back excited. This is the truth. Dr. Marquis had me sit down beside him at his office desk. He chose the schools and filled out the major part of the applications for me in his own hand writing while I looked on. I don't know why he did it. Maybe he sensed I was so ill-informed that I needed help. He'd peer at me through his glasses, "This grad school is rich and has money. Let's apply there."

It has always amazed me that someone, in this case a non-believer, would take such a personal interest in me. Why me? He changed my life! Actually, I think the Lord was leading him to do it. I say that, because I want to encourage you that God has a wonderful plan for your life. Believe it! It may come about in unexpected ways.

Because of Dr. Marquis, I was awarded a TA and scholarship to attend grad school, with free tuition, room and board, plus even some spending money. Altogether, I went on to become a university student for ten years at four different universities (two in Canada and two in the States). I loved the university environment and have never left it.

A final, touching story.

For several decades I did not make any contact with our old teacher, Rowlie Hill. Many years later, I looked up Rowlie and his wife, Clarice, and we had lunch together. He was so excited to see me. We had a great time. Rowlie really dressed up and looked his very, very best, but I could see he was old, fading, and becoming weak.

A year later Rowlie died. Clarice and Rowlie never had children. Clarice told me that Rowlie always talked about Tom and me as, "his boys." She said that he prayed for us daily for decades. To this day, it stirs me to think about it. I felt badly. I had no idea. Why had I not made contact all those intervening years?

If Tom and I have had any success, any ministry worth anything, I believe that Rowlie Hill, our old teacher, had a big part in it.

So these are my last words. Teachers, love your students. Pray for them unceasingly, even if they don't acknowledge you, or look you up.

APPENDIX I
Chord Catalogue

Pop chord symbols are not fully standardized—alternatives exist. This book will be employing (mainly) the symbols in **bold face**, yet you should be aware of other alternatives.

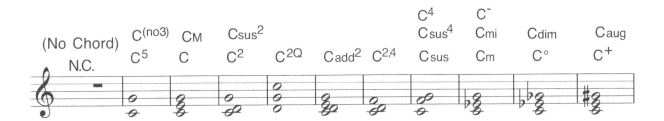

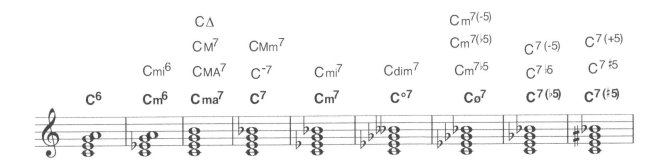

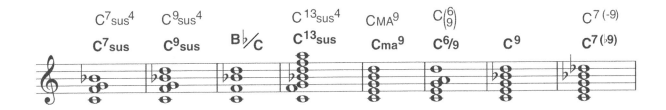

Alternatives to Traditional Harmony

Traditional harmony, expressed by the C chord (135), is composed of thirds, or what is termed "tertian" harmony in classical theory books. Traditional harmony is undergoing an expansion today in contemporary worship music. Sonorities such as 125 and 145 are assuming major roles. These alternatives, which lack the 3rd of the chord, have a more ambiguous sound—they are neither major or minor in quality.

Example 1   Traditional C Chord Compared to Two Contemporary Alternatives

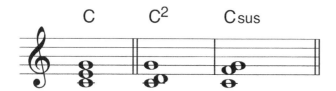

Inversions/Doublings

In measure two, the right hand notes are permutated or inverted. The lowest note becomes the highest note of the next chord. Beat one is in root position. Beat two is in first version. Beat three is in second inversion.

In measure three, various voicings (spacings) occur. The note C of chords two and three is doubled. The fourth chord triples the C (the root).

Example 2

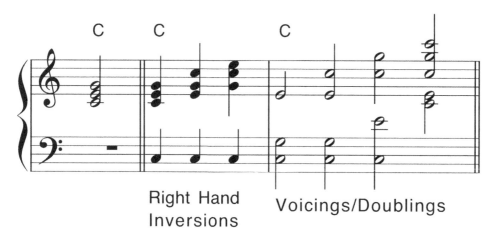

Right Hand Inversions   Voicings/Doublings

Diagonal Slashes

The C/E designation (below) means: play a C chord and a single bass note on E. When slashes are used, the note below the slash always refers to a single note (not a chord). Slashes allow for a division of labor in a band. For example, the guitarist could play the C chord, and a bass player the single note E (an octave or two lower than written).

Example 3

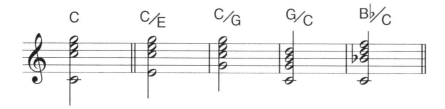

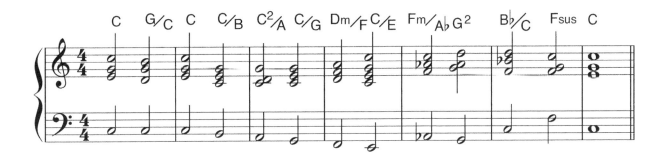

More Than One Spelling

Occasionally a symbol can have more than one spelling. Each pop symbol refers to a fixed sound, but not necessarily a fixed spelling. Chords could be spelled more than one way and yet employ the same symbol. What counts is the number of half steps.

Example 5

The spelling with thirds (m.1) is the default, theoretical spelling, but depending on the musical context, an alternative spelling (m.2) may be appropriate and easier to read.

Example 6

APPENDIX II
Pop Symbols vs. Roman Numerals

Since harmonic issues inevitably arise in keyboard improvisation, you'll find some harmonic explanation below—especially for those not familiar with basic music theory.

Two Worlds—Two Languages

In this book we use music language that is commonly accepted in both popular and classical music circles. Popular/Commercial musicians use pop symbols whereas classical musicians are taught to think in terms of Roman Numerals.

Triads

There are some advantages to Roman Numerals. Below is the C major scale and the triads that result from each scale degree when the collection of notes in the major scale is employed.

Example 1 Triads Derived from the C Major Scale

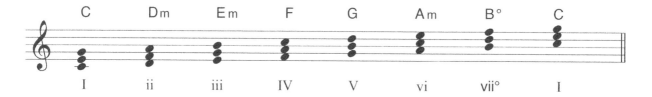

Note that the chords on scale degrees I, IV, and V are major (upper case). Scale degrees ii, iii, and vi are minor (lower case). Scale degree vii is diminished. This chord pattern holds for all major scales (Db, D, etc.), not just C major.

Thinking in scale degrees has a number of advantages, as demonstrated by the example below which transposes a progression of chords from C major to E major.

Example 2 Pop Symbols and Scale Degree Symbols Compared

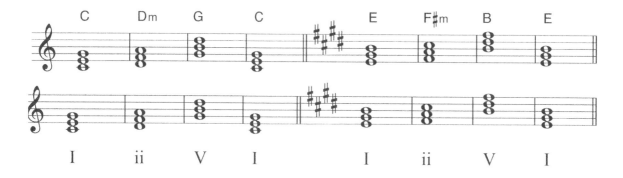

First, note that Roman Numeral designations are more efficient than the pop symbols. The entire line of chords above can be explained by four Roman Numerals whereas eight Pop symbols are required. A single set of Roman Numeral symbols serves both keys.

Second, Roman Numerals help us to think in principles—in generalized ways that apply to all keys.

Third, Roman Numerals give us more information. We learn that the progression of chords 5-8 (above) is the same as 1-4, functionally. This is important information, for in the act of improvising we need to be thinking "in music"—thinking of the function of chords on the fly! Knowing function is vital.

Example 3 Roman Numerals and Triadic Inversions

The symbols for inversions are calculated by the intervallic distance between notes. Below the intervals for each triads are represented above the chord. The symbolic abbreviation commonly used is represented below the chord.

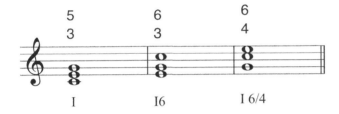

Sevenths

Example 4 Sevenths Derived from the Major Scale

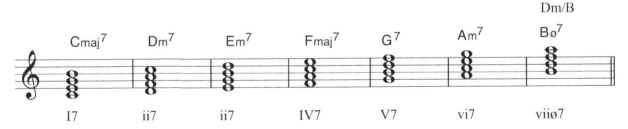

Example 5 Representative Inversions of Seventh Chords

A. Scale Degree One: Inversions of a Major Seventh

B. Scale Degree Two   Inversions of a Minor Seventh

ii7	ii 6/5	ii 4/3	ii 4/2

C. Scale Degree Five   Inversions of a Dominant Seventh

V7	V 6/5	V 4/3	V 4/2

Determine the Root and the Inversion

In traditional music theory, chords are built on stacks of thirds. The lowest third determines the root. Once the root is known it is relatively easy to determine the inversion. If you can understand the logic of the symbols below, you are on your way to understanding how Roman Numerals operate..

Example 6

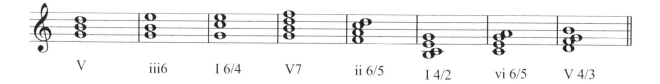

V	iii6	I 6/4	V7	ii 6/5	I 4/2	vi 6/5	V 4/3

Made in the USA
Middletown, DE
08 June 2023

32259078R00124